CAGED BIRD MEDICINE / SELECTED TOPICS

CAGED BIRD MEDICINE

SELECTED TOPICS

CHARLES V. STEINER, JR., D.V.M.
Wickham Road Animal Hospital
West Melbourne, Florida

RICHARD B. DAVIS, D.V.M., M.S.
Department of Avian Medicine
College of Veterinary Medicine
The University of Georgia
Athens, Georgia

IOWA STATE UNIVERSITY PRESS / AMES, IOWA

Printed by The Iowa State University Press, Ames, Iowa 50010

First edition, 1981
Second printing, 1981
Third printing, 1981

International Standard Book Number: 0-8138-1715-3

Library of Congress Card Number: 80-83702

Figures 1.6, 1.9, 1.10, 2.1–2.6, 5.1, 6.1, 10.1, and 10.3 were prepared by Daniel S. Beisel and are copyrighted 1980 by the University of Georgia.

Figures 1.2–1.5 are enlarged adaptations of bird figures presented by Dr. D. R. Collins in "Exotic Psittacines," VM/SAC April 1973, pp. 368–373.

CONTENTS

Contents

ILLUSTRATIONS

TABLES

PREFACE

This syllabus presents the common problems a small animal
practitioner will see when working with caged and aviary birds. It is
not a complete review of caged bird medicine, nor does it offer a
sophisticated approach to every problem. It does, however, provide
the basic information required to diagnose and treat the common
disease conditions of pet birds.

The Authors

CAGED BIRD MEDICINE / SELECTED TOPICS

CHAPTER 1

SPECIES OF CAGED BIRDS

This chapter will familiarize you with the common caged birds and demonstrate how they fit into the overall avian picture. A critical perspective is gained by beginning with the most fundamental classification of the animal world:

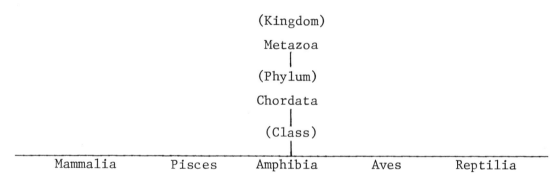

Class Aves is among four others in the phylum Chordata. Within the class Aves there are 27 orders and approximately 8,600 species. Table 1.1 outlines all of the avian orders, listing the common names of representative birds in each order.

Most of our caged birds come from just three orders: the Psittaciformes; the Passeriformes (Fig. 1.1); and two or three species from the Piciformes order. Rarely do we find caged birds from the other orders, but they can be found in private aviaries. A brief discussion of the major species you will encounter in caged bird medicine follows, with emphasis on the size, description, and origin of each. Tables 1.1–1.2 summarize some of this information.

PSITTACINES
    1. Parakeet (<u>Melopsittacus</u> spp.)
    Of all the parakeets only one, the budgerigar (<u>M</u>. <u>undulatus</u>), is kept commonly as a pet. The <u>budgie</u> is also by far the most popular of the caged birds. Originally imported from the drier areas of Australia 100 years ago, the proper name for the budgie is the

<u>Australian</u> <u>Grass</u> <u>Parakeet</u>. It is a slender, long-tailed bird about
7½ inches long with unique barred markings and black-ladder stripes
on the head and back (Fig. 1.2). During the process of domestication,
a number of color varieties have become established, including white,
yellow, blue, and various shades of green. In an optimum environment
its life span is 15-20 years.

Many parakeets are now hatched here in the United States. Male
and female birds look alike except for the cere; the male cere is
blue and the female cere is pink to brown. Also, the feet of males
are bluish-gray while the feet of the female are pink-hued.

Because the parakeet is a flock bird, it is happier if kept in
groups of two or more. Socialization to man is difficult with a group
of birds, but if acquired young and kept as a single bird, many
budgies, with consistent training, learn to talk.

PASSERINE   PSITTACINE

Beak

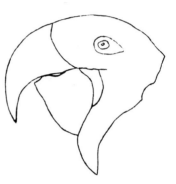

Straight   Curved

Feet

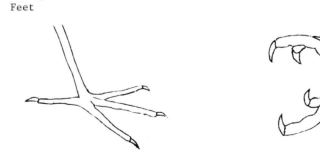

3 up, 1 back   2 up, 2 back

FIG. 1.1. Differences between passerine and psittacine birds.

TABLE 1.1. Orders of the Class Aves

ORDER	COMMON NAMES OF REPRESENTATIVE BIRDS
1. Struthioniformes	Ostriches
2. Rheiformes	Rheas
3. Casuariiformes	Cassowaries, Emus
4. Apterygiformes	Kiwis
5. Tinamiformes	Tinamous
6. Sphenisciformes	Penguins
7. Gaviiformes	Divers or Loons
8. Podicipediformes	Grebes
9. Procellariformes	Albatrosses, Petrels
10. Pelicaniiformes	Tropic birds, Pelicans, Cormorants, Darters, Frigate birds, Gannets
11. Ciconiiformes	Egrets, Herons, Bitterns, Storks, Hammerkop, Ibises, Flammingos, Shoebills, Spoonbills
12. Anseriformes	Screamers, Swans, Geese, Ducks
13. Falconiformes	Vultures, Secretary birds, Hawks, Eagles, Ospreys, Falcons, Falconets, Caracaras
14. Galliformes	Brush turkeys, Guans, Grouse, Pheasants, Partridges, Domestic fowl, Quail, Guinea fowl, Turkeys
15. Gruiformes	Plainswanderer, Cranes, Trumpeters, Rails, Coots, Crakes, Bustards
16. Charadriiformes	Iacanas, Waders (Snipes), Gulls, Terns, Skimmers, Razorbills
17. Columbiformes	Sand Grouse, Pigeons, Doves
18. Psittaciformes	Parrots, Parakeets, Lories, Lovebirds, Macaws, Cockatiels, Cockatoos, Conures, Parrotlets
19. Cuculiformes	Touracos, Cuckoos, Coucals, Roadrunners
20. Strigiformes	Owls
21. Caprimulgiformes	Goatsuckers, Frogmouths, Nightjars
22. Apodiformes	Swifts, Hummingbirds
23. Coliiformes	Mousebirds
24. Trogoniformes	Trogons, Quetzals
25. Coraciiformes	Kingfishers, Motmots, Bee-eaters, Rollers, Hornbills
26. Piciformes	Jacamars, Puffbirds, Barbets, Honeyguides, Toucans, Toucanets, Woodpeckars, Wrynecks
27. Passeriformes	Canaries, Finches, Mynahs, Waxbills, Weavers, Crows, Starlings, Orioles, Birds of Paradise, Buntings, Tree Creepers, Tits, Wrens, Larles, Swallows, Martins, Shrikes, Waxwings, Thrushes, Warblers

TABLE 1.2. Characteristics of the Common Caged Birds

Bird	Size	Special Features	Origin
PSITTACIFORMES			
Parakeet	Small 6–7½"	Long, pointed tail, barred markings	Australia
Parrot	Medium 15"	Short tail	Africa, C. & S. America
Macaw	Large 30–36"	Long, pointed tail	Mexico to Brazil
Cockatoo	Medium 16–18"	Short tail, movable crest	Australia, Solomons
Cockatiel	Medium 12"	Long tail, pointed crest	Australia
Lovebird	Small 6–7"	Short tail, is a small parrot	Africa, Madagascar
Lorikeet	Small 10–11"	Long, pointed tail, a nectar-eater	Australian Islands
Conure	Medium 15–18"	Long tail, is a medium parrot	C. & S. America
PASSERIFORMES			
Canary	Small 5½"	Beautiful song	Europe
Finch	Very Small 4½"	Short, red bill	Australia
Mynah	Medium 12–18"	Large, black bird best talker	India, Ceylon, Burma, Malaysia, East Indies
PICIFORMES			
Toucan	Medium 16"	Huge, light-weight bill; jerky walk	C. & S. America

FIG. 1.2. Parakeet

   2. Parrot (Amazona spp. and Psittacis spp.)
   True parrots come from the southern hemisphere. The familiar
yellow-headed Amazon is found in the tropical forests of Central and
South America. The Amazon is a large bird, about 15 inches long, and
its color is usually a shade of green with some yellow on its head.
The short tail is black, green, and red, there is some blue color in
the wings, and the face is fully feathered (Fig. 1.3). Subspecies,
based largely on color distribution, are the Mexican Double-yellow
Head, the Yellow-naped Amazon, and the Yellow-fronted and Red-fronted
Amazon, to name a few.

FIG. 1.3. Amazon Parrot.

The average life expectancy of the Amazon is 30 to 50 years,
although several birds have lived to be 80 years old. The male and
female look exactly alike and differences can be determined only by
surgery (unless, of course, you see one lay an egg).
There is only one important African parrot, the African Gray.
It brings a very high price because of its excellent ability as a
mime. Like the Amazon, the African Gray is a stout bird, 14-15 inches
long, with a short tail, a round head, and a fully feathered face.

Its tail is a solid red color while the body and head are a bluish-gray. The bill is black. There is no visible difference between sexes.

3. Macaw (Ara spp.)

The Macaw, a very elegant psittacine, measures 3 feet in length, and is found in tropical rain forests from Brazil to Mexico. Several species exist, which may explain why inexperienced breeders pairing two birds of different species are unsuccessful in producing young. The Hyacinthine Macaw is a deep blue all over with a massive black bill. The Blue and Gold Macaw is also blue, but with a green crown and a yellow underside, a white face, gray eyes, and black feet and bill. The Scarlet Macaw, of course, is scarlet with some yellow and blue splashed in. The Military Macaw is OD (olive drab) in color with a red forehead.

Although the macaw measures 3 feet long, the tail accounts for about half of the length (Fig. 1.4). They are very hardy birds and live as long as parrots, but they require considerable attention from humans if they are to be tamed. They thrive on affection and company. In the wild they fly and feed in pairs and experience indicates that solitary birds, whether in the jungle or in a household, rarely survive. A strong perch and a large enclosure are essential.

Macaws will chew anything in sight and their jaws are unbelievably powerful, a fact which should remain foremost in your mind as you perform a physical examination. Like some parrots, they scream if unhappy or frustrated. Their natural voice is harsh and loud, while their speaking voice is soft and pleasant. All things considered, macaws make excellent pets if you have a lot of time to spend with them. However, upon returning from a vacation or other extended leave of absence, do not be surprised to find your bird's breast naked from temperamental feather picking.

4. Cockatoo (Kakatoe spp.)

The cockatoo is a medium-sized (17-18 inches in length) psittacine from Australia, made popular by American soldiers who returned with them from the Solomon Islands and Australia after World War II. Cockatoos are easily distinguished from parrots by their relatively square tail and crest of elongated, pointed feathers which they can raise and lower at will (Fig. 1.5).

White is the common background color of the cockatoo; an example is the bird seen in the television series "Barretta." Pastel overtones can be found on the breast and tail feathers; there are no loud, sharp colors as parrots and macaws sport.

Cockatoos are not noted as talkers but they can be very affectionate, a trait which is demonstrated by the raising of their feathered crest when attention is given by the owner. The most common cockatoos are Leadbeater's Cockatoo, the Sulfur-crested Cockatoo, and the Lemon-crested Cockatoo.

5. Cockatiel (Nymphicus hollandicus)

Next to the budgie, the cockatiel is the most popular psittacine in captivity. It is found in the dry interior of Australia. The cockatiel is slender, measuring 12 inches in length with a long,

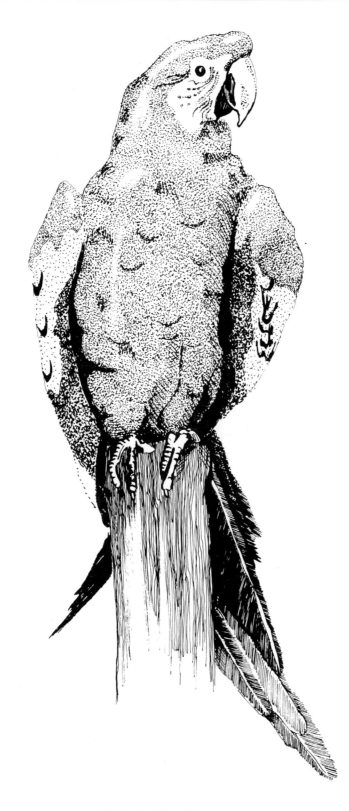

FIG. 1.4. Macaw.

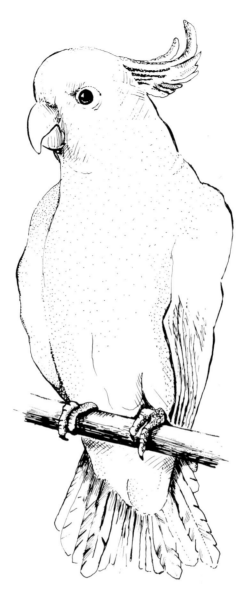

FIG. 1.5. Cockatoo.

tapering tail. The head has a long pointed crest (Fig. 1.6). The
body is soft gray and there are plumage differences between the
sexes. Adult males have a bright yellow face and a circular patch of
orange on the cheeks. Adult females have only a slight trace of
yellow on the face, and the circular patch on the cheek is a much
duller orange than in the male. Males require two years to show their
bright plumage, but their colors begin differentiating at six months.

Cockatiels are the easiest of all birds to breed. They make
excellent pets and can even be caged with other small birds. Their
jaws are relatively weak compared to a parrot; a stoic vet could with-
stand an occasional bite. They are easy to tame and can be trained
easily to mime and do tricks. They do, however, like to whistle

FIG. 1.6. Cockatiel.

loudly when the spirit moves them, a vice some owners find annoying. Breeding stock should not be socialized to humans since the affection-ate cockatiel often pays more attention to an owner than to its mate.

   6. Lovebird (Agapornis spp.)

   The lovebird is a very beautiful psittacine which a novice often perceives as an overgrown parakeet. The bite of a lovebird will quickly change that notion, however. Lovebirds come from Africa and Madagascar. Four species are seen here in America: the Peach-faced Lovebird, the Black-masked Lovebird, the Blue-masked Lovebird, and Fischer's Lovebird. Only the common Peach-faced Lovebird will be described in this discussion.

   All lovebirds are small, short-tailed parrots, 6-7 inches long, and mainly green in color. The Peach-faced Lovebird is light green with a whitish bill, red forehead, peach-colored cheeks and throat, and a blue rump. There is no reliable way to differentiate between the sexes. All species of lovebirds breed freely in captivity. They do not talk and their natural voices are harsh and objectionable. If socialized to man at an early age they become very tame, but they can never be housed with other birds due to a natural aggression directed toward other avian species.

   7. Lorikeet (Trichoglossus spp.)

   A recently popularized psittacine, the lorikeets are nectar eaters from the Australian islands. Using their strong beaks, lori-keets crush fruits and flowers and lap up nectar and juices with a unique brush-fringed tongue. Their plumage is a beautiful mixture of greens, blues, reds, and yellows. They are considered small birds, measuring 10-11 inches in length, half of which is tail.

   8. Conures (Aratinga spp.)

   Conures are long-tailed, small- to medium-sized parrots from Central and South America. They are the most recent psittacine to become popular in America. Along with beauty they have brought with them the scourge of the psittacine world: apparently, conures are the assymptomatic carriers of Pacheco's parrot disease which kills many psittacines every year.

PASSERINES (PERCHING BIRDS)

   1. Canary (Serinis canarius)

   The canary is the second most popular caged bird, its popularity being slightly less than the parakeet but more than the cockatiel. It is really a finch named after the Canary Islands, its place of origin. Throughout Europe in the wild, their high incidence of occurence is noted as greenish-yellow birds with yellow breasts, standing 5 to 5½ inches tall. Through domestication a variety of other colors have developed in canaries. The sexes are alike in appearance and the life span of canaries is 6-16 years.

   Canaries make excellent pets but never yearn for human company like some other birds. They are most often kept for their beautiful melody (only males sing) and pulchritude, so they are ideally suited for a person who likes birds but has little time to fuss over them.

2. Finch (<u>Poephila</u> spp. and <u>Lonchura</u> spp.)

There are several hundred species of Finches and they have a worldwide distribution. Domestic forms are colored gray, tan, cream or buff, occurring as dilutions of the wild type. The wild form is gray and 4½ inches long. The Finch bill is red, the breast white, and the tail black. Males differ from females in that their cheeks are chestnut and their breasts finely barred black and white. Finches are known mainly for their song (Fig. 1.7).

FIG. 1.7. Finch.

3. Talking Mynah (or Myna) (<u>Gracula religiosa</u>)

A member of the starling family, Talking Mynahs are large black birds measuring 12 to 18 inches long, the size varying greatly with the subspecies (Fig. 1.8). The bill and feet are yellow, there is a white patch on each wing, and the sexes are similar. They have no crop, they hop rather than walk, and their life span often exceeds 30 years. Mynahs occur naturally in the tropical forests in India, Ceylon, Burma, the Malay Peninsula, and the East Indian islands.

This species is the best talking-bird around. Unlike the parrots voice, the mynah's comes close to duplicating human tonal qualities. As with all birds, they should start their voice training as young as possible.

The chief drawback to ownership of a mynah is its ability to mess up a cleaned cage in minutes. The mynah is a heavy feeder and its stool is abundant and loose. A minor drawback is that the owner must keep his speech free of undesirable verse lest the mynah, with its great power of mime, repeat the profanity later on.

PICIFORMES

Toucan (<u>Ramphastos</u>)

The Toco Toucan and the Sulfur-breasted Toucan are the most common in captivity. They are beautifully colored with red, white, black, and green colors, but their most striking feature is their

FIG. 1.8. Mynah bird.

huge, soft, light-weight orange bill with dark markings (Fig. 1.9).
The toucan comes from Central and South America and is about 16 inches
long including bill. Males and females are alike.

Toucans are very active birds moving with jerky but precise
movements. Unless the bird is very tame, caging of a toucan can be a
problem because its flight is very awkward. If freightened they often
traumatize themselves in small cages. Toucans are easily tamed, even
as adults, but they have a dominance problem which requires close
monitoring when they are grouped together for the first time.

QUESTIONS
1.   What are the 3 most commonly kept caged birds? List the
     most popular first.
2.   Most of our caged birds come from what two orders?
3.   What birds are in the order Galliformes? Anseriformes?
4.   Name two morphologic differences between a psittacine bird
     and a passerine bird.
5.   What is an example of very small caged bird?
6.   What is the largest of the caged birds and where do they
     originate?
7.   Which pet bird is really a small parrot? Where does it come
     from?

FIG. 1.9. Toucan.

8. Which bird has a short tail and a movable crest?
9. What is unique about the lorikeet? Where does it come from?
10. What are each of the following birds best known for?
    a. Canary
    b. Mynah
    c. Toucan
11. Which bird is probably the messiest of all the caged birds? Why?
12. From memory name the eight most commonly seen psittacines.
13. What is the life expectancy of the parrot?
14. What color is the Military Macaw?
15. Identify the birds in Fig. 1.10 and give the continent of origin.

FIG. 1.10. Silhouettes of common caged birds.

CHAPTER 2

AVIAN ANATOMY AND PHYSIOLOGY

The purpose of this essay is not to present a thorough and complete review of avian anatomy and physiology, but rather to provide the small animal practitioner, who may know very little about a bird, with basic information needed to keep him from looking foolish. Much of avian anatomy and physiology is a carry-over from mammalian anatomy and physiology, but there are many critical differences. These differences will be pointed out and their significance explained in simple terms.

THERMOREGULATION AND THE INTEGUMENT

Birds have an extremely high metabolic rate and the associated problem of temperature regulation. Body temperature of birds varies from 104°F to 112°F with a mean of 107°F. Cooling is accomplished by the respiratory tract and by the skin, although skin cooling is limited by the absence of sweat glands in birds. The evaporation of water from the vast surface area provided by the air capillaries of the lung and the membranes of the air sacs is an effective mechanism for losing heat. When the ambient temperature exceeds tolerable limits, birds frequently extend the neck, gape, and pant with open-mouth breathing to cool themselves down. Prevention of heat loss, on the other hand, is accomplished by the insulation effect of feathers. A bird exposed to cold temperatures or drafts, or a bird which is sick, will fluff or ruffle its feathers and crouch in an effort to conserve heat. Birds with wet feathers and those undergoing a molt are at a disadvantage in conserving heat and should be kept warm, at 80-90°F, and out of drafts.

Bird feathers evolved from reptilian scales and take on five distinct forms:

1. <u>Flight</u> feathers are found on the wings and tail. The lay person knows them as quill feathers. Tail flight feathers are called rectrices and all originate from the pygostyle. Wing flight feathers are called remiges. Both rectrices and remiges have a central axis known as the rachis, which is hollow at its base. From the rachis the feather fans out into a flat vane.

2. <u>Contour</u> feathers are found over most of the body and wings, streamlining and covering the bird while providing insulation and coloration.

3. <u>Down</u> feathers are the small, soft, tufted feathers on short stalks which form the plumage of nestlings and are found under the contour feathers of adults.

4. <u>Filoplumes</u> are hair-like feathers consisting of a very fine shaft with a small tuft of barbs at the tip. Their function is postulated to be one of monitoring proprioception for the larger contour feathers. When an external factor, such as the wind, changes the posture of the larger contour feather, the thin filoplume senses the change by means of free nerve endings in the skin and, via small nerve channels, directs the feather muscles to correct the contour feather posture so as to maintain optimum insulation or proper streamlining for flight.

5. Tiny <u>bristle</u> feathers are found on the face. They have a tactile function in some species and they filter out particles suspended in the air which might enter the nares or eyes and do harm.

As a practitioner, there are four specific points of information you need to know about feathers. The first is that a feather will grow back in 5-10 weeks if you pull the entire feather out, base and all. It will not grow back if only the stalk is cut. This cut feather will be replaced, however, during the normal physiological molt. So, should you need to do surgery, removal of feathers including that part within the follicle to establish a sterile surgical field is an accepted procedure since the feathers will grow back.

The second point concerning plumage is that feathers other than down feathers are arranged in rows or tracts on the integument. If you brush the feathers aside or view a naked bird you will notice that there are wide areas of skin devoid of feathers. This arrangement is normal.

Thirdly, birds undergo a normal loss and replacement of feathers called a molt. Molting is regulated by nutrition (Vitamin A, iodine, B vitamins), age, sex, season, and environment, particularly the photoperiod. Most birds molt one time each year. A few species molt only their primary feathers once but the smaller feathers twice during the year. Psittacines molt continuously throughout the year but may peak in spring and early summer. Passerines in the northern hemisphere, canaries in particular, molt gradually from May to December. Adolescent parakeets molt at 10-12 weeks of age, shedding the cross stripes on their head in the process. In general, 5-8 weeks are required to renew a full complement of feathers.

Finally, the functions of feathers are temperature regulation, protection, sexual attraction, flight, and waterproofing. The waterproofing function is made possible chiefly by the fine structure of the contour feathers. The interlocking of the many small barbules which make up the feather retard the passage of water through the plumage. Waterproofing was thought to be made possible by the secretion of the only gland in the skin, the uropygial or preen gland, located over the last vertebra. Its secretion escapes through a nipple-like protrusion on the dorsum of the tail and is applied to the feathers by the bird's beak during preening. Since birds are able to waterproof their feathers when the preen gland has been surgically removed, its function remains in doubt. The notion that this gland's secretion is a source of Vitamin D_3 precursor, which is spread over the skin during preening and exposed to UV light to form Vitamin D_3, has only recently been disproven.

SKELETON

The notable skeletal modifications which are important to you are listed below:

1. Most bones are pneumatic, containing a pocket of air (a diverticulum of an air sac) surrounded by bone which is thin, hard, and very porcelain-like in its appearance. These bones are much lighter than mammalian bones.

2. Birds have a well developed clavicle.

3. The tail is supported by a fiddle-shaped last vertebra called a pygostyle.

4. There is no costochondral junction in the ribs of birds. Instead, the ribs are attached directly to the sternum by ligaments. The sternum is hinged to permit breathing.

5. The ulna of a bird is larger than the radius.

6. In the wing of a bird, the manus is composed of fused metacarpal bones plus digits 2 through 4. The second digit supports the bastard wing while the third and fourth digits support the primary quills of the wing (Fig. 2.1).

7. A distinct tarsus is absent in the leg of the bird. Instead, the tibia and proximal tarsal bones are fused to form the tibiotarsus, while the second, third, and fourth metatarsal bones and the distal tarsal bones have fused to form the tarsometatarsal bone. The fibula is very reduced in size.

8. In passerines the back toe is digit 1 while the three forward toes are digits 2, 3, and 4 (Fig. 2.2). In psittacines the 1st and 4th digit are in the back while the 2nd and 3rd digits are forward.

MUSCULATURE

Birds are noted for their massive pectoral muscles required for flight. The leg adductors are very weak, predisposing birds to leg problems. There is no muscular diaphragm, but there is a rudimentary, membranous diaphragm. Respiration is brought about by contraction of abdominal and intercostal muscles while at rest and by the action of the pectoral muscles during flight. In most birds, except for psittacines and birds of prey, the muscles of mastication are weak and their bite does not hurt. They will inflict pain during capture, however, by a spearing action with the pointed beak.

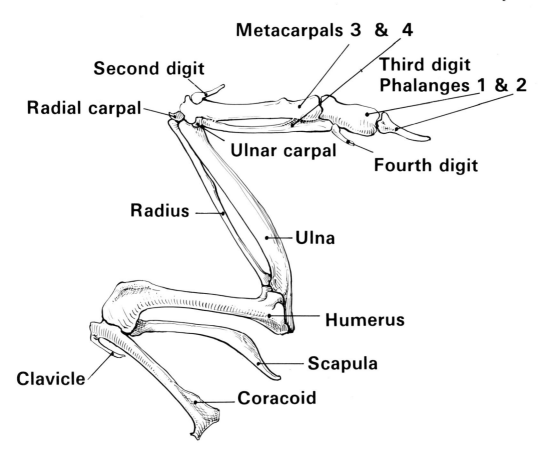

FIG. 2.1.   Left wing, cranial view.

RESPIRATORY SYSTEM
     The lower respiratory system of birds is composed of: a larynx
which has no vocal cords; the trachea; a syrinx at the tracheal bifurcation; primary bronchi; secondary bronchi; tertiary bronchi (or parabronchi); lungs, and a complex series of air sacs. The syrinx is the
voice box in birds and varies from a membranous structure to a very
muscular one. Lungs in birds contain no blind-pouched alveoli for
O_2/CO_2 exchange, but rather there exists a fine network of air (not
blood) capillaries which runs through the lung parenchyma connecting
caudal and cranial air sacs.
     Six pairs of air sacs represent the basic design of air sacs.
There are one pair of abdominal, one pair of caudal thoracic, one pair
of cranial thoracic, one pair of cervical, and two pairs of interclavicular air sacs which communicate with the air spaces in the humeri.
In most birds, the four interclavicular air sacs fuse into one, giving
a total of nine air sacs (Fig. 2.3).

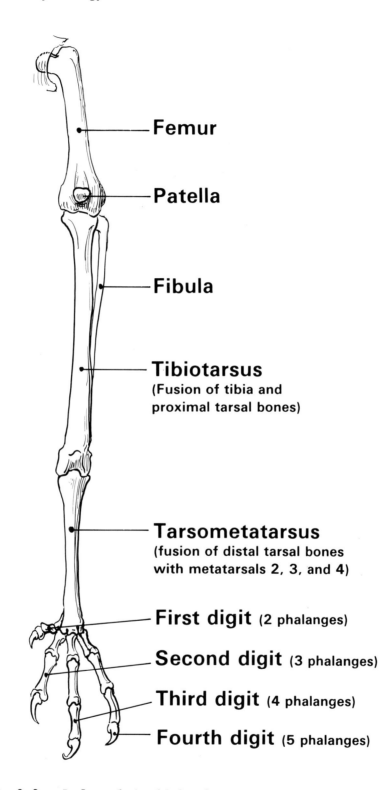

Femur

Patella

Fibula

Tibiotarsus
(Fusion of tibia and
proximal tarsal bones)

Tarsometatarsus
(fusion of distal tarsal bones
with metatarsals 2, 3, and 4)

First digit (2 phalanges)

Second digit (3 phalanges)

Third digit (4 phalanges)

Fourth digit (5 phalanges)

FIG. 2.2. Left pelvic limb of a passerine, cranial view.

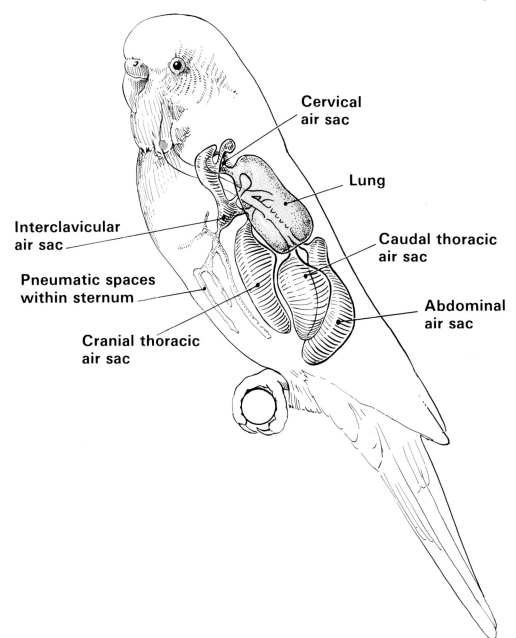

FIG. 2.3. The avian respiratory tree.

HOW BIRDS BREATHE

As previously mentioned, breathing is effected by the action of
the intercostal and abdominal muscles when the bird is not flying.
In-flight breathing is poorly researched for obvious reasons, but it
is believed that the movement of the wings due to pectoral muscle
contraction plays a key role in breathing.

As shown in Fig. 2.4, passage of the air through the respiratory
system is a two cycle process requiring two inspirations and two
expirations for a breath of air to enter and leave the bird. Inspired
air moves from the trachea through the primary and secondary bronchi
into the caudal air sacs, never reaching the air capillaries of the
lung. On expiration this stored air moves cranially through the anas-
tomosing parabronchi of the lungs and into the air capillaries where
O_2/CO_2 exchange occurs. On the next inspiration the air moves from
the lungs forward to the cranial air sacs. With the next expiration
the air passes from the cranial air sacs into the bronchi and trachea
and out of the bird. Once in the bird, then, air moves from back to
front.

Interestingly, the blood flow through the lungs runs exactly
opposite to the air flow, creating a countercurrent mechanism between
blood and air. This countercurrent flow is the key to the bird's
efficient extraction of oxygen, giving it the ability to fly at high
altitudes. Apparently, as air flows cranially through the lungs from

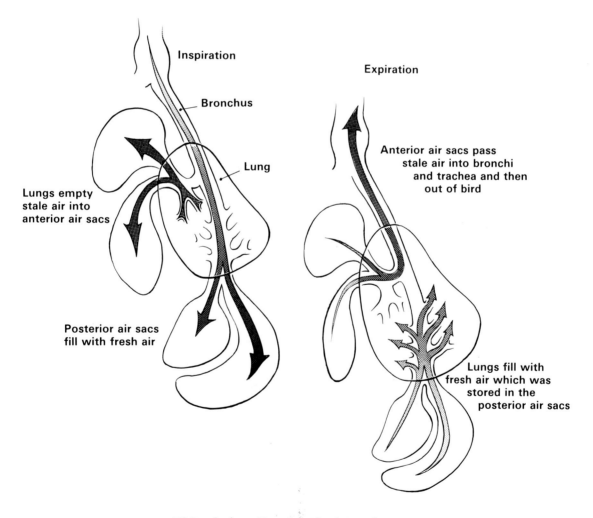

FIG. 2.4. How birds breathe.

the caudal air sacs, blood is moving in a cranial to caudal direction
and can take up more and more oxygen. Furthermore, as blood enters
the lung its pO_2 is very low, creating a partial pressure gradient
with what little oxygen is left in the air as it is about to exit the
lung. As a result, even this residual oxygen is absorbed. Exchange
of oxygen and carbon dioxide does not occur in air sacs.

A recapitulation of what happens during breathing follows:
Inspiration:
   1. Caudal air sacs fill with fresh air.
   2. Lungs empty stale air into cranial air sacs.
Expiration:
   1. Lungs fill with fresh air which was stored in the caudal air
      sacs.
   2. Cranial air sacs pass stale air into bronchi and trachea and
      out of the bird.

A frequently asked board question is, "When does the lung of a
bird fill with air? Inspiration or expiration?" You now know the
answer. It should be mentioned that one non-respiratory function of
the interclavicular air sacs in certain species is that of a secondary
sex characteristic; they can be greatly inflated to give a very
impressive appearance.

DIGESTIVE SYSTEM
   The digestive system of birds has some very specialized organs
and is quite different from that of monogastic mammals (Fig. 2.5).
Since birds have no teeth, most use their lower beak, by raising and
lowering the head, as a scoop for funneling food and water to the
crop. Birds of prey do chop their food into smaller pieces and
psittacines dehull or crack seeds with their beaks. Pigeons and
finches are two domesticated pet birds which can suck. The mouth
of birds contains few taste buds and the saliva, which is basically
enzyme free, functions mainly to hydrate the crop contents. The palate is cleft and totally hard; there is no soft palate.
   Being an expandable organ, the crop or ingluvius serves as a
storage site for ingested food which is awaiting digestion by the
proventriculus, gizzard, and intestine. It is located in the lower
neck on the midline or slightly to the left. In small passerines the
crop is rudimentary while in gallinaceous birds it is very large.
Besides food storage, the crop of the adult parent bird functions in
nourishing the nestling. The epithelial cells of the crop mucosa
swell up and rupture producing a nutritious crop milk which the
adults, both male and female, regurgitate to their young.
   In birds, undigested food in the crop passes through two stomachs
prior to reaching the intestine. The true glandular stomach is called
the proventriculus. As food passes through the proventriculus, hydro-
chloric acid and digestive enzymes are secreted by the digestive
glands. Fish-eating birds possess such potent enzymes that even bones
are digested, while birds of prey, such as owls, cannot tolerate bones
and regurgitate them. Food mixed with digestive juices then moves on
to the ventriculus, the thick-walled muscular stomach or gizzard whose

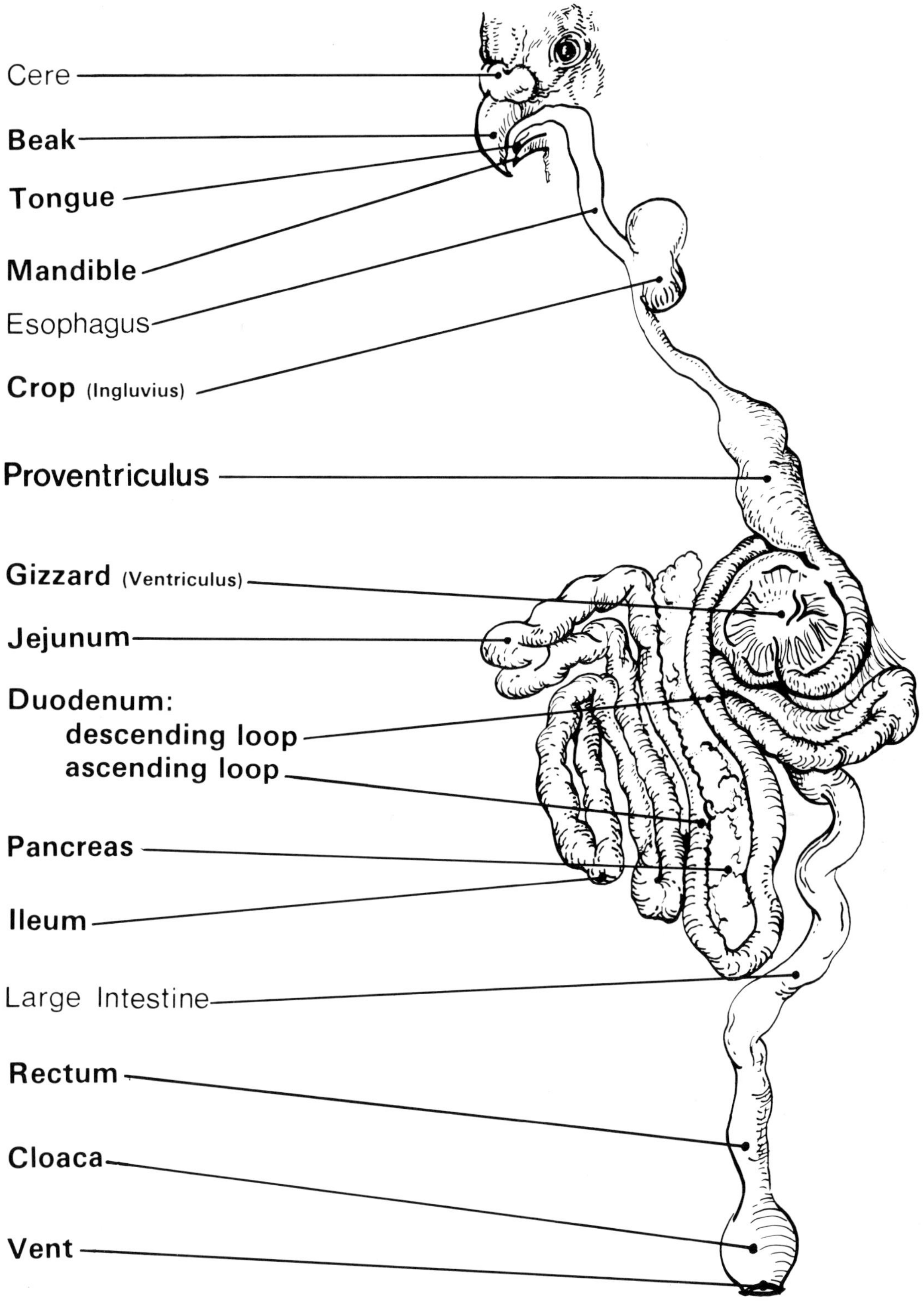

Cere

Beak

Tongue

Mandible

Esophagus

Crop (Ingluvius)

Proventriculus

Gizzard (Ventriculus)

Jejunum

Duodenum:
    descending loop
    ascending loop

Pancreas

Ileum

Large Intestine

Rectum

Cloaca

Vent

FIG. 2.5. The avian digestive tract.

main function is grinding. It is in the gizzard that ingested stone or grit can be found assisting in the pulverization of food particles. A very tough keratin lining called the keratinoid layer serves to protect the gizzard mucosa from all the grinding activity.

The small intestines is a series of fine loops. Within the first or duodenal loop is the pancreas. The supraduodenal loop is the most caudal and is attached to the large intestine which is less than one inch long. The large intestine connects directly to the cloaca.   The cloaca is divided into two compartments: the cranial ventral compartment called the coprodeum, and a caudal dorsal compartment called the urodeum. The coprodeum stores feces while the urodeum collects the semifluid, white urate material from the ureters which empty into it. The exterior opening of the cloaca is the proctodeum or vent.   The duct of the bursa of Fabricius, a lymphoid organ which produces B cells, enters just cranial to the proctodeum. The proctodeum turns inside out during mating in both sexes, permiting the transfer of semen. Birds have no external anal sphincter and consequently possess no control over defecation. When fecal material is presented in large enough quantity to the cloaca, it will soon pass out.

KIDNEYS

Kidneys of the bird are rectangular, reddish-brown, and lobed (Fig. 2.6). They have no cortex or medulla and they are located dorsal to the abdomen in crypts formed by the ribs on either side of the spine, caudal to the lungs. A ureter runs from the caudal lobe of each kidney to the urodeum of the cloaca. Uric acid is the end product of protein metabolism in birds and is excreted by an as yet unknown renal tubular mechanism. Sulfonamides utilize a similar tubular excretory mechanism. Their use in birds must be extremely judicious, especially if there is any evidence of renal damage. A unique system of blood supply to the kidney permits blood from the intestine and legs to pass directly into the kidneys. Clinically, footpad and hock infections or enteritis may quickly result in renal damage if toxins are borne by the blood to the kidney. Therefore, early treatment of these problems is critical.

REPRODUCTIVE SYSTEM

In most birds only the left ovary and oviduct are fully developed. A point of information on which many veterinarians are surprisingly uninformed is that a cycling female can lay eggs without fertilization or mating. Obviously these eggs will not hatch, but they are laid. Mating occurs when the male courts the female and finally mounts her, joining cloacal proctodea which turn inside out. On the dorsum of the male cloacal urodeum is a small mound of tissue called a phallus. The vas deferens, running from the internal testicles, seed sperm into this phallic tissue, which, during mating, further deposits semen into the female's cloacal urodeum where the oviduct begins.

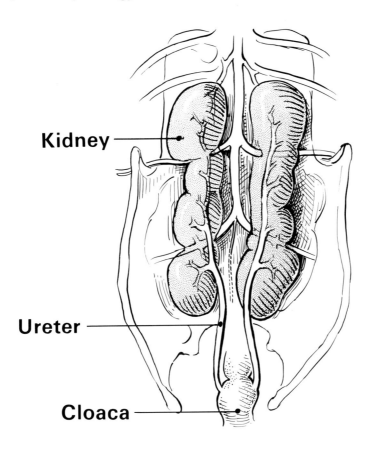

Kidney

Ureter

Cloaca

FIG. 2.6.   The avian renal system.

Other anatomical features of birds include a lymphatic system
with lymphatic follicles in place of lymph nodes, nucleated red blood
cells, no gallbladder in some species, and no external ear. There is
a short, feather-lined ear canal leading to the ear drum.

QUESTIONS
1. How do birds regulate their body temperature?
2. What is the body temperature of birds?
3. Chilled birds should be warmed in an environment which is set
   at what temperature range?
4. Between molts, a feather will grow back if what conditions
   are met?
5. How long does it take for feathers to grow out?
6. What is meant by a feather molt?
7. When do psittacines molt?
8. When does the first molt occur in parakeets? What changes in
   plumage occur at this time?
9. What are four functions of feathers?
10. What is the uropygial gland? What is its supposed function?

11. Why are bones of birds so light?
12. Which bone in birds is larger, the radius or ulna?
13. The tibiotarsal bone (drum stick in chickens) is a fusion of what bones in a mammal?
14. Birds at rest use which muscle for respiration?
15. Which muscles do birds in flight use for respiration?
16. What organ produces the voice sounds in birds? Where is it located?
17. When do the lungs in birds fill with air, inspiration or expiration?
18. Where does the air filling the lungs come from?
19. Where does stale air from the lungs go?
20. The avian lung has no alveoli. Where does O_2/CO_2 exchange occur in the lung?
21. Generally speaking, do most birds masticate?
22. What is the function of the crop?
23. What structures open into the urodeum of the cloaca?
24. What is the name of the copulatory organ of a male bird?
25. Where are the kidneys located in birds?
26. Do birds have:
    a. sweat glands?
    b. a clavicle?
    c. a crop?
    d. teeth?
    e. anal sphincters?
    f. a soft palate?
    g. paired ceca?
    h. alveoli?
    i. a vocal larynx?
    j. significant BUN?
    k. a renal cortex and medulla?
    l. a muscular stomach?
    m. an external ear?
    n. a muscular diaphragm?
    o. nucleated red blood cells?
    p. lymph nodes?
    q. abdominal testes?
    r. a penis?

CHAPTER 3

THE PHYSICAL EXAM

Since even the smallest amount of stress can quickly lead to a serious illness or death, you should make very clear to your clients that you want to see all sick birds no matter how minor the condition may seem. The reason for this is a defense mechanism unique to birds. In the wild, birds are subject to constant predation and must never appear weak or sick, lest they be singled out for attack. Subacutely ill birds, therefore, maintain a nearly normal attitude while using up great energy reserves. When these energy stores are exhausted, the bird's health deteriorates quickly, exhibiting depression, weakness, and anorexia. So, a sick bird is not just becoming sick, it has been ill for some time and is near the end. It is imperative, then, that you see such a bird as soon as possible. The following directions for bringing the bird to the hospital should be given:

1. Bring the bird in its own cage.
2. Do not clean the cage. Bring it as it is so the true environment, especially the droppings, can be examined.
3. Before leaving home empty the water dish and place it back in the cage empty so that no water spills in transit.
4. Remove all grit from the cage.
5. Cover the cage and wrap with a blanket to keep the bird warm, free of drafts, and calm.
6. If the bird is weak, injured, or showing nervous signs, remove any swings and lower the perches.
7. Bring any medicine and vitamin supplements the bird has been taking. A small sample of the seed ration should also be brought in.

HISTORY

Upon arrival at your clinic the bird and its owner should be placed in a quiet, softly lit exam room. While the bird becomes acclimated to his new surroundings, the owner can be filling out a history form by himself or with the aid of a trained assistant (Appendix A). When the form is completed, it should be brought to you (before you ever see the bird) to help you develop an approach to the

31

bird's problem and to suggest what further questions need to be asked. With caged birds, a careful history will provide you with much of the information you need to arrive at a diagnosis.

EXAMINATION OF THE CAGE
       A thorough exam of the bird's cage can provide a lot of useful information about the owner's knowledge of husbandry and the general level of sanitation the bird enjoys. It may even provide clues to the cause of the bird's current problem. Appendix B provides a detailed checklist for cage examination.
       The droppings should be examined first. The bird's excitement, brought on by the new surroundings and the trip to your clinic, will cause him to have several abnormal stools which are wet and tan with no form or shape. These recent stools should be disregarded. The normal parakeet dropping is firm and consists of two parts, the white urates (uric acid) and the dark fecal material. In the stool there should be a central white dot surrounded by a cylindrical black or greenish ring, resembling a small bull's eye. The number of droppings will average 40 in 24 hours but may vary from 25 to 49. A very small stain around the dropping is normal, especially if the bird has greens or fruit in its diet. There is no noticeable odor if the bird is healthy. A decrease in the number of droppings should suggest to you that the bird's appetite is decreased. Droppings pasted to the feathers around the vent suggests the bird is constipated, or that the alimentary canal is obstructed. If the stool is more than half uric acid, renal disease may be suspected, or there may simply be an increase in protein catabolism due to a protein-rich diet or a wasting disease, leading to increased excretion of uric acid. Feces which are green contain considerable bile but the significance of this observation is unknown. Bits of tissue and blood indicate a severe inflammation, usually infectious, in the small or large intestine. Undigested seeds indicate a hypermotile gut or atrophy of the gizzard wall. Some avian clinicians feel that any GI disturbance can cause grit in the gizzard to pass out, leading to poor seed digestion. Simple grit replacement is helpful in these cases.
       Next, observe the feed dish and the cage floor to see what the bird has been eating. If greens, fruits, or vegetables are in the cage check to see how fresh they are or if they are wilted, soft, or spoiled. Look at the mirrors for signs of regurgitation. Mirrors and plastic birds occasionally cause a male parakeet to regurgitate crop milk as part of courtship behavior. Some males will even regurgitate at the sight of their owner. Examine the cage bars and accessories for signs of destruction or chipped paint, and using some magnification device you should scrutinize the ends of the perches and the band around the cuttlebone for mites. They will appear as tiny black dots. You should also insure that the perches are the correct diameter for the bird using them.
       Finally, since the water dish will be empty, be sure to ask the owner about his bird's water consumption. A parakeet will drink from a few drops to 6 ml daily.

PHYSICAL EXAMINATION OF THE BIRD

Before capturing the bird to perform a physical examination, observe it at a distance, noting its attitude, posture, and type of ambulation. Is the bird using its perches or resting on the floor? Is the bird crouching with ruffled feathers or actively moving around the cage? Attempt to gather as much information as possible, keeping in mind that even a very sick bird will perk up when it first sees you. Table 3.1 outlines the general signs of illness to look for in caged birds.

TABLE 3.1.   General Signs of Illness
Talking or singing less, or not at all.
Change in food or water consumption.
Change in the character of droppings.

Change in general attitude:
         Listless
         Sleepy
         ↓ activity
         Lameness
         ↓ flying
 Change in appearance:
         Pasted vent
         Ruffled feathers
         Prolonged molting
         Exudate in and around mouth or eyes

Any respiratory sounds, wheezing, or labored breathing.
Persistent tail-bobbing.
Developing masses in or under skin.

Without fail, you must warn the owner prior to capture about two problems which may occur during capture or shortly after capture:

1. The stress of capture and restraint on a sick bird may cause it to die. Usually this is a chance you and the owner will have to take if a proper diagnosis is to be reached. One way to minimize this problem is to have the owner capture and restrain the bird, which may be less stressful to the bird. Also, if the bird dies, it will have succumbed in the owner's hands, not yours.

2. The second problem, the cardiac racing syndrome, will kill a bird 20 to 30 seconds after you have captured it as you begin your physical. It is a very common problem in parakeets, especially obese parakeets. Out of shear fright the heart rate greatly exceeds normal limits. The heart beats so fast that blood cannot fill the atria and ventricles, drastically reducing cardiac output. Just as you get the bird comfortable in the palm of your hand, it will become quite subdued and go limp. With little blood reaching the brain, the bird faints and finally dies in less than a minute. This phenomenon has

happened to the authors more than once and it is very embarrassing. The client wants to know what you did to kill his bird, and, if you are unfamiliar with the cardiac racing syndrome, so do you. It can happen even with normal healthy birds, so do not reserve your warning to the owner for just the sick ones.

Capture and Restraint

To capture a bird in its cage, remove any perches or toys which the bird may hide behind. Parakeets, canaries, and finches can be easily captured by turning off the lights. These birds will freeze their position, enabling you to catch them. No gloves are needed for these birds, although untamed breeders may necessitate the wearing of a rubber surgical glove since their bite is quite strong (it hurts but won't break the skin). A parakeet is placed in the palm of the hand on its back with the thumb and forefinger secure around the bird's neck just under the head. The little finger can be placed over the legs while the rest of the hand loosely cradles the bird. Do not place your fingers over the bird's breast. It cannot breathe unless the sternum is allowed to rise and fall.

Larger birds require a little more skill to capture. If the bird is civil and can be removed from the cage without flying away or being belligerent, capture is accomplished with a towel. Approach the bird slowly from the rear while someone distracts him from the front. Then throw the towel over him. Quickly and purposefully grasp the bird's mandible with one hand and his feet and trunk with the other. This is no time to be timid or hesitating. The most important hold is the one you have on the mandible. Your hand will stretch around the back of the bird's head while your thumb and fingers secure the lower mandible. A similar capture technique can be employed with the bird inside the cage. You may, however, have to pin the bird against the cage wall or trap him in a corner before you can secure him. Use of leather gloves is a good idea when capturing large birds, but they are not really needed once you learn the towel method. For large parakeets, lovebirds, or small parrots, capture them the same way you would a finch or parakeet (lights off), but wear gloves. They are too agile for the towel in most cases.

The Physical Exam

Before conducting a systematic examination, listen for any respiratory noises and characterize them. Bubbling, rattling, hissing, and squeaking noises all have some significance (see "evaluation of respiratory sounds" in the section on Respiratory Diseases). Then proceed with your physical exam, starting with the head since your initial preoccupation will be with the bird's bite. After the head, examine the feathers and skin, the pectoral muscles, the legs, feet, wings, the abdomen, vent, and preen gland.

When scrutinizing the head of a parakeet, note the color of the cere to determine the sex of the bird. Males have a blue cere while females have a tan to pink cere. Immature birds will not show this difference in color. Breeding females will exhibit a rough-looking

dark brown cere. Also, young birds will have stripes or shell markings on the feathers of the top of the head which extend down to the
cere. These stripes will be lost during the juvenile molt. Immature
birds seem to have larger eyes since there is more black color in the
iris. The iris will become gray with age. Also, the color of the
beak is gray to black in a small percentage of young birds. The cere
and beak should be checked closely for honeycombed crusts caused by
face mites. Often, trauma will cause hemorrhage within the lamina of
the beak, or in the case of some passerines, the tip of the beak will
be blunt or dented somewhat. Examine the bite of the beak for deformity or the need for trimming. "Scissors beak," thought to be an
inheritable defect by some clinicians, is commonly seen in birds not
provided with a cuttlebone. The beak of a parakeet grows ½ inch a
month or 3 inches a year and the curve of the beak should not exceed
90 degrees.

View the eye for pox lesions and check the pupillary response.
If the conjuctiva is injected suspect an infectious problem, either
systemic or localized to the eye. Look for exudate from the nostrils
and see if the infraorbital sinuses are swollen. The external ear or
pinna is absent in birds, but the auditory canal should be examined
for infection or dirt. Using a speculum made from forceps (Fig. 3.1),
pry open the mouth and look for lesions. Vitamin A deficiency produces erosive epithelial disease, Candida and Trichomonas infections
show a thick cheesy exudate, and pox lesions produce scabs and erosions. Check the feathers around the head for evidence of dried
mucus, one indication that the bird has vomited recently. Finally,
part the feathers on the top of the head to look for subcutaneous
hemorrhage, which may indicate a traumatic experience.

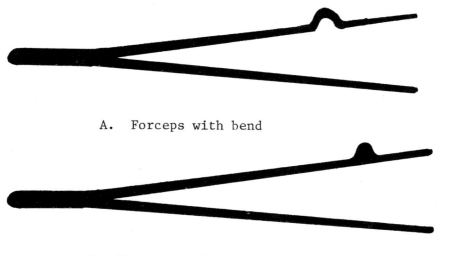

A. Forceps with bend

B. Forceps with solder drop

Figure 3.1. Oral speculums for birds.

   Leaving the head, palpate the crop to see if the bird is eating
or if there is a gross distention suggesting impaction. Foreign
bodies may be discovered through palpating. Hyperplastic thyroid
glands due to an iodine deficiency may possibly be located by palpation at the thoracic inlet, but it is difficult.

   Next, check the condition of the skin and plumage, looking for
mites, lice, tumors, and missing or frayed feathers. Note also how
shiny or dull the feather coat is. Try to determine if the bird is
going through a normal physiological molt, a French molt, or if the
bird is picking itself. Evidence of skin irritation, broken feathers,
or complete absence of entire feathers in areas on the legs, breast,
or under the wing, indicate the bird is picking at itself, probably
due to boredom. In a normal molt healthy pin feathers will be present.
Dull, split, frayed feathers may indicate a nutritional or hormonal
problem. Any broken feathers should be completely removed, the base
included, if the feather is to grow back. The feather base should be
examined under a dissecting scope for evidence of Syringophilus, the
quill mite, which is different from the Megnina species of feather
mite inhabiting the skin and distal parts of the feather.

   French molt is a disease of young parakeets about six weeks of
age. The birds are called creepers and runners since the flight and
tail feathers fail to develop or are weak and defective. The exact
cause of French molt is unknown but there appears to be an association
with overbreeding and poor nutrition. There is no cure for French
molt and the bird should be considered a cull.

   Palpate the pectoral muscles next. Absence of appreciable muscle
mass suggests chronic disease or starvation. At the cranial aspect of
the pectorals near the thoracic inlet, large fat deposits can be
found in obese birds. These fat deposits may even impinge on the
tracheal lumen, compromising respiration.

   The legs should be checked for lesions of Cnemidocoptes pilae,
the yellow subcutaneous urate deposits of articular gout, the feet
abscesses characteristic of bumblefoot (Staphylococcus) infection,
and pox lesions. Spraddle legs, broken down feet due to too large a
perch, and overgrown nails may also be detected. The wings should be
examined for tumors and feather structure.

   The last areas to be examined are the abdomen, vent, and preen
gland. The preen gland may be impacted or show neoplasia, especially
in older birds. A vent pasted with feces or urates is a sure sign of
digestive upset or diarrhea, while thickened skin around the vent is
suggestive of Cnemidocoptes pilae infestation. The key pathological
feature to look for in the abdomen is a sternal lift, indicative of a
space-occupying mass within the abdominal cavity. In parakeets the
distance between the caudal aspect of the keel bone and the pubic
bones is 5 mm. Any measurement greater than 5 mm constitutes an
abdominal lift. It may be caused by a tumor, a bound egg, fat
deposits, or the ascites of heart failure.

   Appendix C, the physical exam form, provides a convenient method
for recording amnesis, pertinent history, and physical exam data.

ROUTINE DIAGNOSTIC PROCEDURES

Body temperature can be measured in birds by inserting a small animal thermometer through the vent and guiding it to the left into the oviduct. The body temperature is so variable that only hypothermia can be considered to be meaningful. Measurement of heart rate should be done with a contact microphone, but a stethoscope over the abdomen can be used. Since the normal heart rate is 300-500 beats per minute, most heart rate determinations will be very unreliable. The really useful information that can be obtained from auscultation of the heart is the presence of heart murmurs or arrhythmias which are common in older birds. Arrhythmias and heart murmurs should suggest the bird may experience exercise intolerance or difficulty in flight.

Blood samples are collected from two sites, the toenail and the wing vein. Using fingernail clippers, a toenail is clipped as closely as possible to the toe. Enough blood to fill two capillary tubes is collected and the toe cauterized with a silver nitrate stick. To collect blood from the brachial vein of the wing, punch a hole in the vein with a beveled needle and collect the blood in capillary tubes as it exits through the skin. Hemostasis in this wound, however, is more difficult to achieve. Keep in mind that the total blood volume of a parakeet and canary is approximately 3 cc and loss of 6 drops or more may place the bird in shock.

The PCV has a range of 42-65 or a mean of 52: any reading less than 40 indicates anemia. Total protein determinations provide a very significant diagnostic measurement. A study by Lafeber (1973) reported that if the value is 2.3 gm/dl or below, death always results despite persistent care. A total protein value less than 4.2 gm/dl indicates a guarded prognosis, while a value of 4.3 gm/dl or above calls for a good prognosis. Other researchers, however, lend confusion to this study by stating that the normal total protein in a healthy bird is 3.8 gm/dl. Our own experience lends credence to the rule that TP < 2.3 gm/dl = death.

OTHER DIAGNOSTIC PROCEDURES COMMONLY USED

1. Radiography. Many birds are small by comparison to pet mammals, so the entire bird can be radiographed on one film. After reading just a few avian radiographs, you will be surprised how easy evaluation is and how much information can be obtained. The major disadvantage is that no bird will remain immobile long enough for a diagnostic radiograph to be taken. Anesthesia is usually required.

2. Cloacal and fecal culture. Mainly for bacterial agents, this tool is discussed in detail in Chapter 7.

3. Fecal flotation. The fundamental procedure for diagnosis of helminth parasitism is fecal flotation.

4. Fecal smear. A fecal smear is especially important for viewing the trophozoites and cysts of Giardia, which is a serious problem in caged and aviary birds although it is reported infrequently.

5. Abdominocentesis. Abdominocentesis is valuable for diagnosis of peritonitis, neoplasia, and ascites, but be careful not to damage abdominal air sacs during the procedure.

6. <u>Cytological examination</u>. Cytological examination of ante-mortem and postmortem lesions aids in the diagnosis of avian pox, tumors, gout, xanthomatosis, psittacosis, etc. Stained smears of exudate and affected tissues are simple to prepare and evaluate and are quite informative.

7. <u>Blood smears</u>. The presence of blood parasites can be demon-strated by blood smears.

After arriving at a diagnosis and administering therapeutic agents give the pet bird owner specific guidance for convalescence of the bird at home. Appendix D offers detailed instructions to an owner taking his bird home from the hospital.

QUESTIONS

1. Why should a client not clean his sick bird's cage before coming to your clinic?
2. Describe the normal parkeet dropping (stool).
3. How may the droppings of an excited bird just entering your clinic appear? Are these droppings significant?
4. How many droppings will a healthy parakeet produce in 24 hours?
5. What could cause a decreased number of droppings?
6. Why should you examine a bird's mirror?
7. Where should you look for mites in a cage? What do they look like to the naked eye?
8. How much water does a parakeet drink in a 24 hour period?
9. What can you learn by observing a bird at a distance in its cage before capturing it?
10. What two warnings must you give the client prior to capturing his bird for a physical exam?
11. How do you hold a parakeet?
12. What important precaution must you take when holding a parakeet?
13. How do you capture a large psittacine?
14. How can you determine the sex of parakeets?
15. How can you differentiate immature and mature parakeets?
16. What information does palpation of the crop provide?
17. How can you differentiate feather picking from molting?
18. What is the French molt? What type and age of birds are affected?
19. What conditions should be considered when examining a bird's legs and feet?
20. What is the main thing to check for when examining a bird's abdomen?
21. Where do you draw blood from a bird for PCV and TP measure-ments?
22. What is the normal hematocrit range in pet birds? When is a bird considered anemic?
23. At what level is the total protein considered normal? Irreversibly low?

CHAPTER 4

NUTRITION OF CAGED BIRDS

Without question, the literature concerning what diet should be offered caged birds is filled with the most varied and contradicting reports ever seen. It is indeed quite reasonable that birds of the same species prefer the different rations detailed by so many authors: a bird's eating habits from birth influence his choice of foods. If given a variety of foods during early, impressionable months, a bird will be more likely to favorably consider a diverse ration as an adult. Birds placed on a narrow seed diet, as is the case with birds raised by wholesalers, will usually reject any different or new food offered by a new owner.

Choice of food is also influenced by its appearance and the bird's personality. Birds have a poor sense of smell and taste but can see very clearly. They quickly become accustomed to their diet and any change is met with considerable skepticism and suspicion. Color of feedstuffs apparently plays a key role in this element of avian behavior. The authors have noticed that by consistently using a yellow water dish and then switching to a blue one, the bird's water consumption will decrease dramatically for a few days until the bird becomes accustomed to his new colored dish. Finally, the personality of different birds within a species may play a role in what new foods they will accept, just as some humans have an aversion to eggplant, squash, or spinach. Personality is probably molded somewhat by the effects of heredity but most certainly by experience.

DIETARY REQUIREMENTS
In general, birds require 7 types of materials in their diet:
1. Fats
2. Carbohydrates
3. Proteins
4. Vitamins
5. Minerals and trace elements
6. Grit
7. Water
Only a small amount of fat is required since most caged birds lead

39

such a sedentary life that they manufacture considerable fat from the carbohydrate-filled seed diet they eat. A minimal quantity of dietary fat is critical, however, so that fat soluble vitamins can be absorbed and essential fatty acids are made available. In the wild, birds eat a lot of varied foods but burn up the calories' quickly. In captivity the lack of exercise, coupled with doting owners who feed the bird what it likes instead of what it needs, leads to obesity, a major cause of illness in caged birds. Sunflower seeds and peanuts contain considerable fat and should be a small part of a ration or used as treats.

Proteins are critical for optimum growth in caged birds. In general, plant proteins have a lower biological value than animal proteins, the protein content of cereal grains being relatively low. Table 4.1 lists the essential amino acids required by the chicken, which we will assume are similar to those required by caged birds since so little research has been done in caged bird nutrition. These essential amino acids must be present in the ration because the bird is unable to synthesize them from other amino acids in the body.

TABLE 4.1. The Essential Amino Acids Required by the Bird

Arginine

Lysine

Histidine

Leucine

Isoleucine

Valine

Methionine

Threonine

Tryptophan

Phenylalanine

Vitamins required by birds are the fat-soluble vitamins, A, D, and E, the water soluble vitamins, the B complex vitamins, and vitamin C. The following vitamins must be provided in the diet:

1. Vitamin A--does not occur in plants. Carotene is ingested and converted to vitamin A which is stored in the liver. Seeds have no carotene so it must be supplied as a supplement or from other parts of plants (leaves and stems).
2. Vitamin B_1 (thiamine)--cereal seeds are a good source.
3. Vitamin B_2 (riboflavin)--synthesized only by green plants. Vitamin B_2 is readily available in cereal seeds.
4. Niacin (nicotinic acid)--synthesized in the animal from the essential amino acid tryptophan. Adequate niacin, therefore, is dependent upon adequate tryptophan in the diet.
5. Vitamin B_6 (pyridoxine)--green leafy materials and whole grains are excellent sources.
6. Pantothenic acid--green leafy plants are a good source but seeds are not. Pantothenic acid is a constituent of coenzyme A.
7. Biotin--found in green leafy plants, peanuts, and eggs. Cereal grains are a poor source of biotin.

8. <u>Choline</u>--fish meal and fish oils contain choline. Soybean meal is also a good source but it is goitrogenic if uncooked.
9. <u>Folic acid</u>--found in green leafy materials and seeds.
10. <u>Vitamin C</u> (ascorbic acid)-- not required by most species, but may be required by fruit and nectar-eating birds which may possibly be unable to synthesize it.
11. <u>Vitamin D</u>--specifically vitamin D_3 (cholecalciferol). Vitamin D_3 is required for the synthesis of a hormone which permits production of calcium-binding protein. Fish oils and eggs are the main sources of vitamin D_3 (see chapter on Rickets). An all seed diet will be deficient in vitamin D_3 in addition to vitamin A.
12. <u>Vitamin E</u>--present in seed germs. Vitamin E deficiency may be caused by excessive cod liver oil or unsaturated fatty acids which cause oxidation of vitamin E.

Vitamins K and B_{12} (cyanocobalamin) are synthesized by microorganisms in the digestive tract and are not required in the diet. Table 4.2 correlates various avitaminoses in birds with pathological findings.

The minerals and trace elements required for optimum growth, maintenance, and egg-laying are calcium, phosphorus, magnesium, sodium chloride, manganese, zinc, iron, selenium, and iodine. All seed diets will be deficient in calcium and iodine. Calcium can be obtained from a cuttlebone, ground oyster shells, or bone meal. Iodine is abundant in fish oils or it may be provided by adding one to two drops of Lugol's solution to the drinking water per week. Seed-eating birds also require grit in free choice amounts to aid the gizzard in grinding food. A mixture of several different stone sizes should be offered to the bird who will chose which is best for him. Parakeets prefer grit which is 1 mm in diameter. About 100 grains are usually present in a parakeet at a given time.

Physiologically birds require slightly less water than mammals because they do not sweat and because nitrogenous wastes are eliminated as insoluble uric acid rather than as water-soluble urea. Evaporative cooling through the respiratory tree does place a significant demand on water, however, and seed-eaters like the canary and finch have a critical need for water. Many caged birds are able to extract water from succulent foods, while budgerigars even utilize metabolic water to some degree. Generally, all birds should be supplied with ample fresh water (except the nervous over-drinker which takes in so much water it develops chronic diarrhea).

In Tables 4.3-4.7 at the end of this section, we present a balanced diet for large psittacines, small parrots, parakeets, canaries, and nectar-eating birds. Care should be taken to check the feed dish daily and not confuse hulls and seed parts with whole, uneaten seeds. A cuttlebone (squid backbone), mineral block, and a synthetic multivitamin supplement are required for all birds. Cod liver oil can be added at the rate of one teaspoon to a pound of seed. This mixture should be refrigerated, if stored, since cod liver oil oxidizes quickly and becomes rancid.

TABLE 4.2. Vitamin Deficiencies in the Bird

Vitamin	Clinical Activity
Vitamin A	epithelial damage in skin, respiratory, digestive and reproductive tracts; changes in eye function
Vitamin D	rickets; soft-shelled eggs
Vitamin E	degenerative myopathy, encephalomalacia, exudative diathesis
Vitamin K	reduced clotting ability
Vitamin B_1 (thiamine)	polyneuritis, anorexia, poor digestion, weakness
Vitamin B_2 (riboflavin)	curly toe paralysis
Niacin (nicotinic acid)	poor growth, poor feathering, perosis, and scaly dermatitis
Vitamin B_6 (pyridoxine)	anorexia, weight loss; ↓ egg production and hatchability; microcytic, hypochromic anemia
Pantothenic acid	retarded growth, poor feathering, dermatitis, granulation of eyelids, necrosis around mouth and on feet, liver damage, ↓ hatchability
Biotin	perosis, poor hatchability, dermatitis
Folic acid	macrocytic anemia, perosis, poor feathering, retarded growth
Vitamin B_{12} (cyanocobalamin)	retarded growth, poor hatchability
Choline	perosis (slipped gastrocnemius tendon)
Vitamin C (ascorbic acid)	possibly scurvy in nectar and fruit-eating birds

TABLE 4.3.   A Balanced Ration for the Amazon, African Gray,
             Cockatoo, and Macaw

1. Seed Mixture: 1/3 quality large canary seed
                    1/3 mixed sunflower and safflower seed
                    1/3 mixed cereal seeds and nuts
                          1 part ground nuts (shelled or unshelled)
                          1 part sweet corn
                          1 part milo or dari
                          1 part buckwheat
                          1 part rolled oats

2. Protein Supplement:

    A. Small amounts of ground or chopped meat, either fresh or from
        a can of all-meat dog food.

                              OR

    B. Non-medicated chick starter ration (poultry food)--bird may
        not eat it unless chopped, cooked egg or a freshly grated
        carrot is added.

3. Fruits and Vegetables: every bird prefers a different combina-
    tion; attempt to vary the combination to prevent a "narrow"
    ration from developing.

    A. Fresh foods:
        apples   oranges   bananas   plums   grapes
        pears   grapefruit   figs   dates

    B. Dried fruits may be substituted for the above fresh fruits.

    C. Grasses and leafy vegetables*:
        chickweed   spinach   cabbage
        plantain   endive   lettuce
        dandelion leaves   carrots

4. Nuts: Macaws love to crack open and eat a variety of nuts,
    especially Brazil nuts. Other large psittacines also like nuts,
    each bird preferring a specific kind. Amazons and African Grays
    love peanuts.

    * Never forget to wash insecticides off fresh vegetables. Keep
birds away from flowers and houseplants, especially geraniums, philo-
dendrons, and cacti. Do not feed candy, biscuits, etc. Remove all
uneaten fruits and vegetables at day's end to prevent ingestion of
spoiled food and soiling of plumage.

TABLE 4.4. A Balanced Ration for Small Parrots, Conures,
and Large Parakeets
_____

1. Seed Mixture*:   50% quality large canary seed
                     25% mixed safflower and sunflower seed
                              1 part large white millet
                              1 part hemp
                     25% - 1 part dari or milo
                              1 part buckwheat
                              1 part hulled oats

2. No Protein Supplement Required.

3. Fruits and Vegetables:

    A. Fresh foods:

        apples   oranges   bananas
        plums   pears   grapefruit
        figs   dates   grapes
        sweet, ripe cherries raspberries   logan berries
        blackberries   fresh green oats seeding chickweed

    B. Dried raisins, currants, and nuts can be given in place of
        fresh fruits.

4. Millet Sprays: these birds will eat a millet spray when they
    won't eat anything else.

_____

    * A premixed, commercial seed mixture is available for this type
of bird. You should be aware, however, that many feed mills use the
cheapest, lowest quality seeds for their mixture. The quality of the
individual seed types seems to become obscured when viewed as part of
the total mixture, so on paper the ration appears adequate. We
suggest purchasing the seeds yourself and preparing your own mixture.

TABLE 4.5.   A Balanced Ration for Parakeets, Lovebirds,
Small Conures, and Dwarf Parrots

1. Seed Mixture: The basic seed mix contains canary seed, millet,
   and hulled oats.

       50% mixed canary seed or white canary seed
       25% mixed millet seed (no red millet)
             1 part sunflower
       25% - 1 part safflower
             3 parts hulled oats or rolled oats

Canary seed should be increased in juvenile rations, while millet
should be increased in the adult ration. A commercial seed ration
which contains millet and canary seed in either a 60/40 or 40/60 ratio
is available. Also, spray millet is very popular with parakeets.
Parakeets will consume 1-18 gms of seed per day.

2. Protein Supplement: crumbled, hard-cooked egg yolk.

3. Greens: chickweed   spinach   cloves
             dandelion   carrot tops   rye grass
             sowthistle   alfalfa   beet tops
             watercress   brussel sprouts   celery leaves
             cabbage leaves   broccoli   kale

Feeding greens presents a dilemma which you and your bird will have
to work out together. When presented with greens, some birds will
wolf down every leaf in sight and develop diarrhea. The solution is
to offer small amounts over a long period of time. Offering greens
once daily for ½-1 hour and then removing them, as recommended by
some experts, may be an answer to this problem, but more often than
not it just teaches the bird that he had better eat while he can, so
he consumes a lot in a short time and develops diarrhea.

4. Vegetables: carrots   beets
               turnips   parsnips

5. Fruits: apple   orange   grapes   figs
            grapefruit banana   pineapple   pear

Never leave fruits in the cage overnight. They will spoil quickly
and cause diarrhea if ingested.

TABLE 4.6. A Balanced Ration for Canaries and Finches

1. <u>Seed Mixture</u>: 50% canary seed

                        25% rape seed

                        25% mixed millet

                              2 parts yellow millet
                              1 part white millet
                              1 part red millet

A seed treat of niger seed, poppy seed, flax seed, sesame seed, oats,
and anise is available commercially and can be offered periodically.
These seeds are fattening, however.

2. <u>Greens</u>: Fresh, washed kale, lettuce, spinach or dandelions
    should be offered daily.

3. <u>Protein</u>: cooked egg
              cooked egg combined with biscuit mix

4. <u>Carbohydrate</u>: plain biscuits - crumbled

5. <u>For Parents Feeding Young</u>: sprouted seed

                                  seeding grasses

                                  live food - maggots, mealworms,
                                      termites, Drosophila

TABLE 4.7. A Balanced Ration for Fruit and Nectar-eating Birds

In the wild, lories, lorikeets, toucans, and toucanettes feed on nectar found in flowers, insects found in the nectar, and sweet, ripe fruits.

1. Nectar formula:

    a. Mellin's food . . . . . . ½ teaspoon
        Honey . . . . 1 tablespoon
        Condensed milk . . . . . 2 teaspoons
        Boiling water . . . . . . 5 tablespoons

Allow to cool and add two to four drops of multiple vitamin supplement. Mellin's Food is a maltose dextrin mixture containing thiamine, ferric glycerol phosphate, and potassium bicarbonate. This ration must be prepared fresh daily and twice on hot days to prevent spoilage.

        OR

    b. Baby cereal . . . . 1 part
        Semolina . . . . 1 part
        Wheat germ . . . . 1 part

Mix with thin honey until a crumbly consistency. Vitamins may be added. This preparation will not cause loose droppings and it does not readily spoil. Refrigeration is not necessary. Add water for smaller birds to make eating easier.

2. Sweet, ripe fruits: can be offered in a separate dish or small amounts can be mixed into the nectar formula.

    Fresh fruits softened by overnight soaking in water
    Berries
    Canned fruit salad
    Canned baby fruits

3. Insects: mealworms intended for fish can be soaked and added to the nectar formula.

4. Other treats:

    A. Wild rice boiled in milk with brown sugar and honey added.
    B. Fruits mixed with mashed potatoes.
    C. Fruit cake, sponge cake, or wheat bread soaked in milk and honey.

5. Greens: when possible offer dandelions, spinach, lettuce, celery, or beet tops.

The rations described are complete and balanced. They will
properly nourish the growing adolescent, the egg-laying hen, and the
regurgitating parent. Also, you should be especially cognizant of the
unbalanced diet received by young, growing birds at ports of entry and
wholesale houses. To control disease they are given chlortetracycline
impregnated millet for several weeks. A diet of millet only will not
permit optimum growth. New owners, therefore, should correct this
poor situation as soon as possible.

QUESTIONS
1. What factors influence a bird's choice of ration?
2. What are the seven materials birds require in their diet?
3. Why are only small amounts of fat required in caged bird rations?
4. What is the relative protein content of cereal grain - high or low?
5. What vitamins are fat-soluble?
6. What compound is vitamin A made from? What part of a plant contains lots of this compound?
7. **What vitamins are synthesized by microorganisms in the GI tract?**
8. Do birds need vitamin C?
9. What is a good source of vitamin D_3?
10. Why do birds need grit?
11. Which bird can make use of metabolic water to some degree?
12. What is a cuttlebone?
13. How can you be deceived when checking a feed dish and finding it full?
14. How is malnutrition created in young growing birds by a wholesaler?
15. Describe two protein supplements for large psittacines.
16. Why wash fresh fruits and vegetables?
17. What two vitamins are most likely to be deficient in all seed diets?
18. What two minerals are most likely to be deficient in all seed diets?
19. How can calcium be supplied to parrots and parakeets?
20. How should grit be supplied to birds?
21. A seed diet contains what basic type of food?
22. What 3 seeds does the basic seed mix for parakeets contain?

CHAPTER 5

CHEMOTHERAPY FOR CAGED BIRDS

Medicating caged birds is accomplished by the same methods of administration used in mammals, but with several special points kept in mind. Birds which are seriously ill, in shock, or moribund simply will not tolerate handling or injections very well. The stress of your capture and injection is usually enough to kill a really sick bird. But such a bird will probably die if not medicated, so go ahead and administer the drug as gently as possible. Also, very little research has been conducted on drug efficacy, dosage, and blood levels in caged birds. Most of our knowledge consists of practitioner reports. Response to therapy, therefore, is not always consistent.

Another critical point is that the use of a drug in one avian species does not mean it can be used safely in another species, or the dose for one species is the same as for another. Most drug reports use the parakeet and canary as models, with extrapolation for larger species.

The following outline will point out the significant advantages and disadvantages of the major methods of drug administration in caged birds: drinking water; oral dropper; gavage; feed, and intramuscular injection. Other less frequently used methods will also be mentioned.

MAJOR METHODS OF DRUG ADMINISTRATION
1. <u>Medication in the Drinking Water</u>
   Advantages -
   - a. Can use on large numbers of birds without individual treatment.
   - b. Easy to prepare and administer.
   - c. Can give drugs orally which are tissue toxic.
   - d. Dose need not be as exact as parenteral dose.
   - e. Good for medicating large birds like the parrot and macaw.
   - f. No stress of capture and restraint.
   Disadvantages -
   - a. Many medications have a bad taste or they color the water, causing most birds to stop drinking. The bird then becomes more dehydrated and more ill.

49

b. There is a variable taste preference among birds of the same species.

c. The parakeet is originally a desert bird, able to utilize metabolic water, and is suspicious of any beverage other than pure water.

d. Unsure of amount of water consumed.

e. Must monitor bird to see if it drinks.

f. Unsure of blood levels of drug.

g. Desired blood level reached slowly.

h. Drug must be water soluble.

i. Drug must have a wide margin of safety if bird is an excessive drinker or polydipsic.

See Table 5.1 for a basic list of oral medications.

2. <u>Dropper</u> - use a plastic dropper, never glass, and offer a volume which does not exceed the crop capacity of the bird. The size of the drop is important. Use small drops for very small birds.

Advantages -

a. Easy to administer.

b. Good for alimentary tract infections

c. Doses don't need to be as exact as parenteral doses.

Disadvantages -

a. Birds have an agile tongue and often refuse to swallow. Some medication is lost.

b. Blood levels of drugs are uncertain.

c. Desired blood levels of drugs are reached slowly.

d. Aspiration pneumonia occurs if drug is administered too fast.

e. Must capture and restrain bird → stressful.

f. Small birds are limited in the amount they can drink.

3. <u>Gavage</u>

Method -

a. Materials:

1. Tuberculin or 3 cc syringe for a parakeet.

2. Needle - 16 gauge with point cut off to give 1.5 inch length.

3. Polythylene tubing - PE #160, ID = .045 inches, OD = .062 inches, length 2 inches. Heat tubing in hot water and seat snugly over flat bevel of needle.

4. Use appropriate-sized French catheter for larger birds.

b. Using digital pressure or soldered forceps, pry open the bird's mouth.

c. Pass tubing over the back of the tongue and gently insert into esophagus and down into crop. The natural S-shaped curve of the cervical vertebral column should be straightened by gently stretching the neck. <u>Never</u> force the tubing down the esophagus.

TABLE 5.1. Basic Oral Medications

	Strength	A/U*	Dosage
Tetracycline (Lederle)	100 mg/ml	A	350 mg/pint H_2O (1 tsp/8 oz H_2O)
Chlorhexidine (Fort Dodge/Nolvasan)	---	U	1 ml/quart H_2O for 5 days
Chloramphenicol (Parke-Davis)	100 mg/ml	A	320 mg/pint H_2O (12 drops/oz H_2O)
Tylocin (Tylocine/Pitman-Moore)	50 mg/ml	A	200 mg/pint H_2O (12 drops/oz H_2O)
Lincomycin (Aquadrops/Upjohn)	100 mg/ml	A	200 mg/pint H_2O (6 drops/oz H_2O)
Amoxicillin (Amoxidrops/Beecham)	50 mg/ml	A	.25 ml/30 gm body wt. BID (4 drops/oz H_2O)
Carbenicillin indanyl Na (Geocillin/Roerig)	500 mg tablet		Crush ½ tablet and mix with 4 oz H_2O; use as sole source of drinking water
Erythromycin (Abbott)	200 mg/ml	A	200 mg/pint H_2O (3 drops/oz H_2O)
Kanamycin (Kantrim/Bristol)	50 mg/ml	U	125 mg/pint H_2O (8 drops/oz H_2O)
Spectinomycin (Spectam/Abbott)	100 mg/ml	U	125 mg/pint H_2O (4 drops/oz H_2O)
Mycostatin Oral Suspension (Squibb)	100,000 units/ml	U	.25 ml/30 gm body wt. BID
Testosterone (USP)	25 mg/ml	A	1 drop/oz H_2O for 30 gm bird
Dexamethasone (Azium/Schering)	1 mg/ml	A	3 drops/tsp H_2O
Lugol's Iodine	---	A	1 drop/8 oz drinking H_2O for 3 wks
Sulfadimethoxine (Bactrovet/Pitman-Moore)	100 mg/ml	A	1 drop/30 ml drinking H_2O
Allopurinol (Zyloprim/Burroughs Welcome)	100 mg tablet	A	Crush and mix with 10 ml H_2O; add 20 drops to 1 oz H_2O
Metronidazole (Flagyl/Searle)	250 mg tablet	A	.05 mg/gm p.o. SID for 5 days; is toxic to finches
(Emtryl/Salsbury Labs)	---	A	1 tsp/gallon of drinking water for 5 days; halve the dose on hot days.

* Absorbed or unabsorbed (across the gut).

    d. Deliver a volume which does not exceed the crop capacity of the bird:

Parakeet	1 ml
Canary	.25 ml
Finch	.1-.5 ml
Cockatiel	2-4 ml
Small Parrot	3-6 ml
Lovebird	1-10 ml
Medium Parrot	10-15 ml
Large Parrot	20 ml

Advantages –

    a. Equipment for gavage is cheap and easy to construct.

    b. The exact amount of medication consumed is known.

    c. Can give tissue-toxic medications.

    d. Good for alimentary tract infections.

    e. Most birds require fluids and nutrients when sick. Anorectic parakeets will die in 48 hours. Include medication with nutrient and fluid supplement.

        1. Nutrition and hydration - give BID or TID
            -3 parts Neo-Mulsoy^R (or any hypoallergenic soybean food for infants).
            -1 part Gevral^R protein supplement
            -Add vitamins A, B, D_3, E.

        2. Collapsed bird - give 5% dextrose every half hour for 3 doses, then give the supplement described in 1 above.

Disadvantages –

    a. Must exercise strict sanitation of gavage apparatus.

    b. Bird may regurgitate if crop filled quickly.

    c. Must capture and restrain the bird, particularly large ones.

    d. Small birds require extreme care in delivering proper volume into the crop.

4. <u>Medicated Feed</u>

Advantages –

    a. Can be used on large numbers of birds without individual therapy.

    b. Chlortetracycline (CTC)-impregnated seed (Keet-Life^R) is available commercially.

    c. Good for infections sensitive to CTC like psittacosis.

    d. No stress of capture and restraint.

Disadvantages –

    a. Since CTC-impregnated millet is all that is available, you can use this method only on infections sensitive to CTC.

    b. Certain seed-eating birds leave the impregnated millet in the dish.

    c. Unsure of amount of medication ingested.

    d. Must monitor to see if bird eats.

    e. Unsure of blood levels attained.

    f. Desired blood level reached slowly.

      g. No commercial preparation available for nectar-eating birds or non-seed eaters like the Mynah.

      h. Parakeets dehull seeds with beak, discarding the impregnated hull.

      i. If you mix in your own medication, it nearly always settles out.

5. Intramuscular Injection

      a. IM is the easiest and most preferred method.

      b. Use tuberculin or microliter syringe.

      c. Must weigh bird for precise dosing.

      d. Injection site: pectoral muscles.

      e. The needles must be sharp. A dull or burred needle causes enough trauma to kill a sick bird.

      f. Ensure there is no blood loss from the injection site. Loss of six drops or more in a small bird will put it in shock.

See Table 5.2 for basic IM medications. Table 5.3 lists those drugs which are contraindicated in caged birds.

The Microliter Syringe

      a. Maximum volume: 100 microliters or 0.1 ml.

      b. Needle size: Use 25 or 26 gauge, 3/8 inch-long disposable needle.

      c. There is almost zero clearance between the plunger and barrel. Do not handle carelessly or lubricate with material of a viscosity greater than that of water.

      d. Always clean immediately after use and sterilize.

      e. Available as Model #710 from The Hamilton Company, P. O. Box 17500, Reno, Nevada 89510.

Advantages - IM injection

      a. Once bird is restrained, medication is easy to administer.

      b. You are certain of the exact amount the bird receives.

      c. Desired blood levels are reached quickly.

Disadvantages - IM injection

      a. Special equipment required (microliter syringe). It is expensive and requires special care.

      b. Must sterilize microliter syringe since it is not disposable.

      c. Many medications are toxic to muscle tissue.

      d. Bird must be captured and restrained → stressful.

      e. Must know precise weight of the bird.

OTHER METHODS OF DRUG ADMINISTRATION

1. Subcutaneous Injection

      a. Used mainly for fluid therapy to rehydrate birds which are too sick to drink.

      b. Amino acid preparations are also delivered by this route.

      c. Injection site: axilla, skin of neck, groin.

TABLE 5.2. Basic Parenteral Medications

	Mfg.	Route	Strength	Vol/gm Body Wt.	Vol/30 gm parakeet
Tetracycline (Achromycin)	Lederle	IM	100 mg/ml	.00085 ml	.025 ml (2.5 mg)
Chloramphenicol succinate (Chlormycetin succinate)	Park Davis	IM	100 mg/ml	.00034-.0005 ml	.01-.015 ml
Gentamycin (Gentocin)	Schering	IM	50 mg/ml	.00034 ml	.01 ml
Tylocin (Tylocine)	Pitman-Moore	IM	50 mg/ml	.00034-.00068 ml	.01-.02 ml
Spectinomycin (Spectam)	Abbott	IM	100 mg/ml	.0013-.002 ml	.04-.06 ml
Kanamycin (Kantrim)	Bristol	IM	50 mg/ml		
Sulfadimethoxine (Bactrovet)	Pitman-Moore	IM	100 mg/ml	.00024 ml	.007 ml
Dexamethasone (Azium)	Schering	IM	1 mg/ml	.0002-.00068 ml	.006-.02 ml
Testosterone	USP	IM	50 mg/ml	.001 ml	.03 ml
NaI	USP	IM	20%	.00034 ml	.01 ml

TABLE 5.3. Drugs Contraindicated in Caged Birds

Procaine*
Procaine penicillin*
DDT
Streptomycin**
Dihydrostreptomycin**   } → > 1 mg/20 gm body weight

    * These drugs can be used if administered in sensible doses. The problem is that haste may cause preparation of an improper dilution or use of a syringe that is too large, two conditions that have disastrous results for very small birds.
    ** These antibiotics are less than effective, especially when compared to the other broad spectrum antibiotics available. Their use is not recommended.

    d. Skin of bird lacks elasticity and fluid will often run back out.
    e. Volumes to be delivered subcutaneously:

Parakeet	1-1.5 ml
Cockatiel	3-3.5 ml
Parrot	5-10 ml

2. Intravenous Injection
    a. Difficult to accomplish in small birds.
    b. Good restraint required.
    c. Injection site: jugular vein or wing vein.
    d. Hematomas form easily and may throw small birds into shock.

3. Intraperitoneal Injection
    Not recommended. You may fill up an air sac.

4. Intranasal Injection
    a. Used to deliver antibiotics (for sinusitis) and decongestants.
    b. Be certain medication is of low viscosity and does not occlude nares.

5. Intrasinus Injection
    a. Used to irrigate infraorbital sinuses with saline and antibiotics in chronic sinusitis.
    b. Holding a low, beveled needle with syringe at an angle between the eye and the naris, place the needle through the skin in the area caudal to the commissure of the mouth, directing the needle ventral to the zygomatic arch, no more than 2 mm into the sinus (Fig. 5.1). When the sinus is infused, excess fluid will exit via the nares. Since the sinuses of psittacines are connected, excess fluid may be seen leaving both nares. If this happens, the contralateral sinus will have already been filled and will not need to be flushed directly. In passerines, however, there is no connection and bilateral injections are necessary. If a sharp, beveled

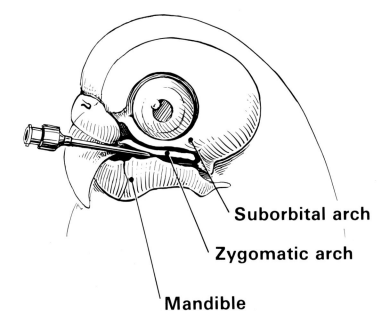

Suborbital arch

Zygomatic arch

Mandible

FIG. 5.1. Direct a low beveled needle ventral to the zygomatic
           arch to a depth of 2 mm.

           needle is used and the improper injection site used,
           considerable trauma to the eye will occur if the ocular
           orbit is punctured.
6. Ophthalmic (topical)
    a. Used to deliver antibiotics and steroids for conjuncti-
        vitis.
    b. Must be given frequently requiring restraint and pro-
        ducing stress.
    c. Ointments are difficult to deliver because the 3rd eye-
        lid interferes: aqueous solutions are sure to reach the
        cornea.
7. Conjunctival Injection
    a. Used to treat conjunctivitis.
    b. Blebs last 24 hours.
    c. Do not exceed 0.1 ml in parakeets.
8. Topical
    a. Bird will nearly always ingest medication.
    b. Use Elizabethan collar.
    c. Principal use is in therapy of external parasites.
9. Inhalational Route (nebulization)
    a. Uses:
        (1) Humidifies and soothes inflamed respiratory
             epithelium.
        (2) Respiratory therapy - add antibiotic and deconges-
             tant to saline vehicle. A satisfactory level of
             antibiotic is delivered topically to the respira-
             tory epithelium but there is no systemic absorp-
             tion.

(3) Air sac mite treatment – atomize malathion.
   b. Place nebulizer in incubator with bird or place bird, if small, in nebulizing jar.
   c. More primitive method involves placing bird in bag with powdered medication and thumping the bag to stir up the powder, for example, 5% carbaryl dust for air sac mites.

QUESTIONS
1. If you medicate a moribund caged bird with a proven drug at the proper dosage and the bird dies, what is the most probable cause of death?
2. What is the easiest and most preferred parenteral method of drug administration?
3. What are the sites of injection for the following routes of drug administration?
     a. IM
     b. IV
     c. SubQ
4. Where can you obtain a microliter syringe?
5. Concerning the microliter syringe:
     a. What is the maximum volume of the syringe?
     b. What size needle should be used?
     c. What part of the milliliter is a microliter?
6. What medicated feed is available commercially?
7. What are the major drawbacks to placing medication in the drinking water of parakeets?
8. Describe how you would gavage a parakeet.
9. What is the maximum volume that should be delivered by gavage to the crop of a parakeet?
10. What are the principal uses of inhalational therapy?
11. Describe where to make an intrasinus injection.
12. Bilateral intrasinus injections in psittacines showing bilateral sinusitis are not always required. Why?
13. What precaution must be taken when using topical therapy in caged birds?
14. What limits the usefulness of subcutaneous injections in caged birds?

CHAPTER 6

DISEASES OF THE RESPIRATORY SYSTEM

A. Introduction
B. The Respiratory Examination - Signs
    1. Sustained, increased respiratory rate.
    2. Tail-bobbing.
    3. Signs of effortful breathing.
    4. Heavy-lidded, sleepy bird.
    5. Huddling and ruffling of the feathers.
    6. Signs of upper respiratory tract involvement.
    7. Abnormal respiratory sounds.
        a. Hissing or whistling in head
        b. Click in head or neck
        c. Bubbling, roaring, rattling over trachea
        d. Cough or sneeze followed by a gulp
        e. Loss of voice, dyspnea, explosive chirping on
            expiration
        f. Low pitched hiss or roar near thoracic inlet
C. Rhinitis - Characterize the Exudate
    1. Serous.
    2. Proliferative encrustations.
    3. Catarrhal.
D. Sinusitis
E. Larynx, Trachea, Syrinx, and Bronchi
    1. _Trichomonas_ and _Candida_ in larynx.
    2. Laryngotracheitis and Newcastle disease.
    3. Trachea and bronchi.
        a. Avian pox
        b. Irritant gases
        c. _Syngamus trachea_ - the gapeworm
        d. Thyroid hyperplasia
        e. Nonspecific tracheobronchitis
F. Air Sacs
    1. Inhalation of irritant gases.
    2. Infectious airsacculitis.
    3. Air sac mites.
    4. Subcutaneous emphysema.

G. Lungs
    1. Congestion - significance.
    2. Pneumonia.
H. Treatment Philosophy
    1. Standard therapy.
    2. Nebulization therapy.

     Respiratory problems in birds are very different from those of
mammals. The respiratory system itself differs both anatomically and
physiologically, and auscultation and percussion of the respiratory
tree is very difficult. In fact, it is almost impossible to hear the
lungs which are shielded by thick pectoral muscles ventrally and ribs,
bones, and back muscles dorsally. The greatest problem birds face,
however, is the lack of a mucociliary apparatus in the air sacs. As
you know, the continuous beating movements of cilia towards the oropharynx, aided by the secretion of a mucus blanket over the mucosa,
permit the expulsion of foreign material, infectious agents, and exudate. In the bird this apparatus exists down to the major bronchi
but not in the air sacs. As a result, the very sensitive air sacs,
when inflamed, become coated with a heavy, thick exudate which has no
place to go.

THE RESPIRATORY EXAMINATION
     Since most caged birds are small, the physical examination of the
respiratory system is often difficult, imprecise, and unrewarding.
What you must do then is become familiar with the signs of respiratory
disease which birds exhibit.
     1. Sustained, increased respiratory rate. Whenever possible a
bird should be examined at long range, in its own environment, or
after 24 hours of hospitalization. If your client owns an aviary, you
probably will satisfy all of these conditions. As you know, sudden
exercise or apprehension in humans causes an increased respiratory and
heart rate. If the person is in good physical condition, both return
to normal within minutes. If poorly conditioned, the respiratory and
heart rates remain elevated for quite some time. Birds respond similarly. When a stranger approaches, you can sense the apprehension in
birds, whose respiratory rate and body activity increase 20-50%.
Within 10 to 60 seconds, depending on the size of the birds, their
composure and normal respiratory rate are regained if the birds are
healthy. (Normal respiratory rates are listed in Table 6.1.) An
unhealthy bird, however, will continue to breathe quickly and show the
signs discussed next.
     2. Tail-bobbing. The cardinal sign of respiratory disease,
tail-bobbing can be seen with exertion or apprehension even with the
slightest respiratory involvement. If the bird has severe respiratory
involvement, tail-bobbing will be noticed at rest. The bird usually
must be perching, however, to observe tail-bobbing. This presents a
problem in birds with such severe respiratory involvement that they
rest on the floor where the tail is supported and not allowed to bob.

TABLE 6.1.   Respiratory and Heart Rates of Caged Birds

	Respiratory Rate (Per Minute)	Heart Rate (Per Minute)
Macaw	55-78	120-220
Parrot	36	140-200
Parakeet	80-100	250-600
Conure	44	240-260
Lovebird	120-132	260-280
Mynah	22-50	110-192
Canary	96-144	560-1000
Finch	120-190	600-1000

Tail-bobbing is a physiologically normal response to overheating, anxiety, handling, and exertion, but ceases when these factors are eliminated.   Persistent tail-bobbing, then, is a sign of respiratory disease.

3.   Signs of effortful breathing.   Especially if obstructive lesions of the upper part of the respiratory tract exist, signs of effortful breathing may be seen, such as heaving movements of the thorax and intermittent or continuous gaping.

4.   Heavy-lidded, sleepy bird.   In true pneumonic conditions (lung involvement) an oxygen deficit will exist despite increased rate and depth of respiration.   The main sign will be that of a heavy-lidded bird which keeps nodding off to sleep.   Such a bird will be hypercapneic and unable to find the energy to perch.   It will huddle on the floor of the cage with eyes closed and head drooping if undisturbed.   Since the tail will be supported by the floor, a tail-bob cannot be observed.

5.   Huddling and ruffling of the feathers.   These signs are not specific for respiratory disease but are nearly always present with respiratory involvement.

6.   Signs of upper respiratory tract involvement.   In birds, noisy breathing, sneezing, nasal exudate, swollen sinuses, ocular discharge, and conjunctivitis are usually associated with conditions of the upper respiratory tract just as in mammals.   Gaping and neck extension are seen in obstructive lesions of the larynx and trachea.

7.   Abnormal respiratory sounds.   Best auscultation is accomplished by a contact microphone but a conventional stethoscope can help if you practice a lot.   Considerable information can be obtained just by positioning yourself close to the bird and listening while it rests.

a.   Hissing or whistling in head - dry, partially obstructive lesions of the nasal passages, accompanied by visible external evidence of dried exudate.

b.   Click in neck or head - nearly complete upper respiratory obstruction or exudate is thick but movable.

c.   Bubbling, roaring, rattling over trachea - obstructive lesions of glottis and trachea.   In severe cases gaping occurs with only slight exertion, or continuously if death is imminent.

        d. Intermittent cough or sneeze, preceded or followed by a
gulp - trichomoniasis, candidiasis, Syngamus infection, aspiration of
crop contents or irritant gases, or foreign bodies in larynx or
trachea.

        e. Loss of voice, change in vocal pitch, dyspnea, or explo-
sive chirping on expiration - pressure on the lower trachea or syrinx
by hypertrophied thyroid glands, local neoplasia, or enlarged heart.
The slightest stress in such cases produces extreme distress, gaping,
and sudden death.

        f. Low-pitched hiss or roar near thoracic inlet - thoracic
airsacculitis. The abdominal air sacs are also likely to be involved.
Respiration is deeper, accelerated, and more effortful than normal.
If the exudate within the air sac becomes so thick that it is raised
by the rapid passage of air, a click can be heard over the lower neck.

    Lung sounds are so difficult to interpret that we choose not to
discuss them. As a matter of fact, it is almost enough to make association between an abnormal sound and the respiratory system itself,
since most respiratory conditions require standard antibiotic and
symptomatic therapy. Exceptions are sinusitis, which involves intrasinus flushing with antibiotics, Syngamus infections of the trachea,
thyroid hyperplasia, pleural gout, and air sac mite infection. So
practically speaking, do your best to localize the problem in a specific area of the respiratory tree, but if the condition is too generalized, treat symptomatically. Very often, abdominal tumors, eye problems producing an ocular discharge, or an impacted crop will be confused with a respiratory problem because of similar signs. Experience
and a careful examination will help you in your diagnosis.

    We will now turn our attention to conditions affecting specific
areas of the respiratory tract.

RHINITIS (cere, nares, nasal passages, and palatal cleft)
    In rhinitis look for exudate and characterize it, since all
insults are calculated to produce an exudate.
    1. Serous - pox, other viruses, and Mycoplasma infections. Pox
lesions may be dry and scabby or wet and serous. Distribution of
lesions is common over the face, head, and mucous membranes. They are
brought on by stress, the pox virus being transmitted by insects. Pox
lesions compromise respiratory passages and debilitate the bird, causing eventual death in many cases. Occasionally a bird will survive
the infection which lasts several weeks. Prevention of secondary
bacterial infections with antibiotics offers the only hope of dealing
with pox. Mycoplasma infections are diagnosed by culturing exudate.
They respond to tetracycline or chloramphenicol therapy.
    2. Proliferative, encrustations on the face and beak - Cnemido-
coptes pilae infestation, if unchecked, may cause crusts of hyperkeratosis to overgrow the nares and block the passage of air.
    3. Catarrhal - Candida and Trichomonas infections actually
originate in the oropharynx or crop, with the tenacious mucoid exudate
spreading to the nares. So look in the mouth if you see a catarrhal

exudate. Another possible source of catarrh might be spread of the exudate from a catarrhal sinusitis.

Abscesses due to the presence of pyogenic bacteria, as a rule, do not form. Instead, obstructive granulomas are seen. Other non-exudative lesions also exist in the turbinates. Obstructive neoplasms, foreign bodies, especially regurgitated material, arthropod bites, and erosive, necrotic, ulcerative lesions which produce a foul odor, are examples.

Therapy for obstructive lesions involves removal of the obstruction by excision or curretage followed by application of a topical antibiotic cream or ointment, taking great care not to occlude the nares. Supplemental oral or parenteral antibiotic therapy is optional. Mosquito or other arthropod bites causing undue facial swelling and respiratory distress should be treated with antihistamines and dexamethasone.

SINUSITIS

Infraorbital sinusitis is very common in large parrots and mynahs, but has been seen in all caged birds. It is either a local infection or a manifestation of an upper respiratory tract or ocular infection. Occasionally sinusitis is initiated by fighting.

The causative agent is either bacterial, fungal, or mycoplasmal. The bacterial agent is usually staphylococcus, but culture of the exudate should certainly be done. Hemophilus infection, the causative agent of infectious coryza in domestic fowl, may play a role in caged bird sinusitis but reports are scant, mainly because Hemophilus is so difficult to culture. Often when bacterial cultures are negative, Mycoplasma in conjunction with a viral infection is suspected. The fungal etiology is nearly always Aspergillus.

The bird commonly presents with a swelling below one or both eyes. The swelling can be firm or fluctuant and if large enough may push the eyeball dorsally as the bone of the orbit becomes distorted by the exudate in the infraorbital sinus. Signs of sinusitis associated with a systemic disease include reddening of the face below the eye, a serous catarrhal, or mucopurulent discharge from the nares and eyes, sneezing, head-shaking, head-hanging, closed eyes, and anorexia.

Localized sinusitis is treated by intrasinus irrigation with saline, which flushes out the exudate, followed by injection of the appropriate antibiotic. Gentamycin is extremely effective. Inspissated exudate must be removed surgically. The sinus is curretted, flushed chemically cauterized with QAC or 4% aequous silver nitrate, and filled with an aequous antibiotic of choice. If the sinusitis is secondary to a systemic problem, systemic antibiotic therapy should also be instituted.

Parrots showing sinusitis are given a special treatment. Immediately upon diagnosis of sinusitis, daily IM injections of chloramphenicol succinate [(0.03 ml/100 gm (concentration of chloramphenicol is 100 mg/ml)] are given for 7 days. The bird should also be placed in a nonstressful environment at 85°F with a heating pad and regular circadian light for a minimum of one month. After 30 days, if the bird

responds to therapy the temperature can gradually be returned to room
temperature. Intrasinus irrigation with saline and antibiotics is
optional, as is administration of aequous ophthalmic solution of
gentamycin or chloramphenicol in the nares.

LARYNX, TRACHEA, SYRINX, AND BRONCHI

The larynx may show trichomoniasis or candidiasis as an extension
from a fullblown oropharyngeal or ingluveal infection. The tenacious,
cheesy exudate may occlude the laryngeal lumen or be aspirated into
the lungs. Trichomoniasis has been treated effectively with dimetridazole, while Candida infections have been treated with nystatin.

Laryngotracheitis (LT), a highly infectious viral disease of
domestic fowl, has not been noted to be a problem in caged birds.
Similarly, Newcastle disease (ND), the scourge of the poultry industry, is not very common in most caged birds but should always be look-
ed for. Serological surveys indicate that many caged birds have been
exposed to ND or are assymptomatic carriers of the virus. Practically speaking then, the trachea and bronchi of pet birds exhibit five
disease conditions:

1. Avian pox - caused by any one of several avian pox viruses.
Exudative lesions with occasional diphtheritic membrane formation
cause the problem. Also, the respiratory epithelium is eroded, per-
mitting infection by opportunistic bacteria. Eosinophilic intracytoplasmic inclusion bodies can be found in tracheal epithelial cells
during the early stage of infection. The pox virus is transmitted by
insects and the lesions, precipitated by stress, generally debilitate
the bird and cause death. Vigorous antibiotic therapy can help in
some cases.

2. Irritant gases. Exposure to ammonia, aromatic hydrocarbons,
paraffin (kerosene) vapor, volatile aerosols, and caustic agents such
as lye (oven cleaners) causes effusive sero-catarrhal exudate to form
in the trachea and bronchi. Chronic exposure may lead to epithelial
erosion and hemorrhage of the mucosa. Bubbling, rattling and possibly
sneezing are the common signs. This condition will most often occur
iatrogenically when you or the owner attempt to treat air sac mites
with a volatile insecticide or try to kill tracheal gapeworms with
sodium fluoride powder. Removal of the causative agent and providing
a nonstressful environment are the best treatment. Humidification via
nebulization is also helpful.

3. Syngamus trachea infections - a nematode, commonly known as
the gapeworm. Transmission is either direct by ingestion of infective
eggs or larvae from the soil or indirect by ingestion of paratenic
(transport) hosts such as earthworms and snails. From the GI tract of
the bird, the larvae migrate to the trachea where the adult female
attaches to the tracheal mucosa. The smaller male permanently
attaches to the female, giving the pair of worms a Y-shaped appearance, and breeds. In response to irritation by the worms, the bird
produces excess mucus and coughs and sneezes violently in an effort to
dislodge the parasites. During these bouts of coughing, the eggs are
coughed up, swallowed, and pass out in droppings, becoming infective

in 1-2 weeks. Small birds are the worst affected since the worms and mucus can actually occlude the trachea. Other signs include throwing the head forward, head shaking, and gasping for breath. Often a bird will become exhausted and die from inability to take in food or water.

Nestlings are the most prone of all birds, especially in a large aviary with a soil floor. Adult birds will regurgitate food to the young or bring the infected transport host for lunch, infecting their offspring.

Diagnosis of gapeworm infection is by signs and fecal flotation. The gapeworm egg is pictured in Fig. 6.1. Treatment involves the oral

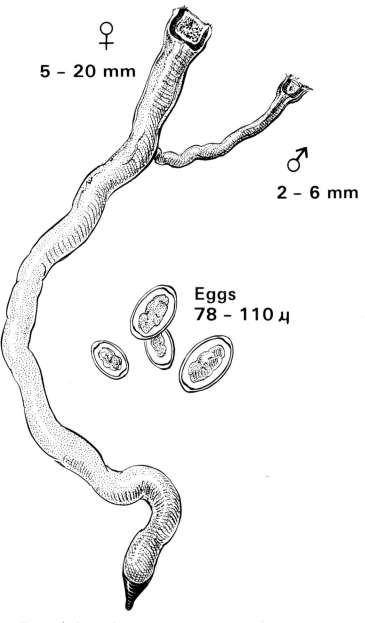

♀
5 - 20 mm

♂
2 - 6 mm

Eggs
78 - 110 µ

FIG. 6.1. The gapeworm, _Syngamus trachea_.

administration of thiabendazole (TBZ) at the rate of 50-200 mg/kg for
7-10 days, but the birds, especially small ones, may have trouble
coughing up the worms. Levamisole 40 mg/kg can also be given in a
single dose subcutaneously. In larger birds, the beak can be pried
open and a soft cotton swab gently inserted into the trachea. A
twisting motion on withdrawal will remove many of the worms.

    4. _Thyroid hyperplasia_. The thyroids are located about ½ cm
cranial to the tracheal bifurcation on either side of the trachea. A
diet deficient in iodine will inhibit the production of thyroxin
causing the thyroid to become hyperplastic in an effort to increase
the falling blood level of thyroxin. Normal thyroids measure ½ mm x
1-2 mm, while hyperplastic thyroids may be enlarged up to 10 times
the normal size and can be palpated during a physical exam. As the
thyroids enlarge, they may impinge on the trachea or syrinx, causing
a violent chirping on expiration or just simple respiratory distress.
Therapy involves mixing two drops of Lugol's iodine per ounce of
drinking water for 2 to 3 weeks. Advanced cases often die.

    5. _Nonspecific tracheobronchitis_. The causative agent may be
bacterial, viral, or mycoplasmal. A combination of a viral and mycoplasmal infection precipitated by stress is very common. The respiratory epithelium of the trachea and bronchi becomes hyperplastic and
there is excessive mucus production. Dyspnea, coughing, and rattling
are the signs. Treatment with systemic antibiotics is effective if
the therapy is instituted early enough.

AIR SACS

    Before covering the specific disorders of air sacs, we will ex-
plain the pathogenesis and complications of air sac pathology. The
air sacs are lined by a single layer of epithelial cells which undergo
marked inflammation in response to an insult. As previously mentioned, exudates produced by inflamed air sacs have nowhere to go, forming
an excellent medium for invading pathogens. Any accumulating fluid,
whether it be blood, ascites, or exudate, will eventually spill over
into the air capillaries of the lung, drowning and asphyxiating the
bird. Prevention of iatrogenic drowning by accumulation of blood or
serous fluid during or after surgery can be accomplished by making all
surgical approaches to the abdomen and thorax on the ventral midline
so as not to rupture the bilaterally symmetrical air sacs. The notion
that inflamed air sacs cannot exchange oxygen and CO_2 is irrelevant
since the air sacs do not have an exchange capability.

    There are four basic air sac disorders in caged birds: air sac
mites; infectious airsacculitis caused by variety of pathogens; subcutaneous emphysema, and inflammatory airsacculitis due to inhalation of
irritant gases.

    1. _Inhalation of irritant gases_ of any type, including dense
cigarette or cigar smoke, will inflame and thicken the air sacs.

    2. _Infectious airsacculitis_ is caused chiefly by _Aspergillus_,
E. coli, _Mycoplasma_, _Pasteurella_, Newcastle disease virus, and
Chlamydia psittaci. Generally, you won't know which is the cause un-
less a culture is taken on necropsy. The infections can be acute with

little or no gross lesions, or eventually consolidate the air sacs
with exudate. The signs, even with heavy consolidation, may be non-
existent until sudden death occurs. Usually, however, the bird will
appear normal at rest but show dyspnea, collapse, and death on flight.
Sounds from the diseased air sacs may be heard by auscultation as a
click or bubble as air passes over the exudate. Chronic airsacculitis
presents a bird in poor condition.

    Aspergillus is the only etiologic agent you can tentatively diag-
nose on necropsy. Focal white, cream, yellow, or green masses (fungal
granulomas or pearls) will be seen. Dextrose Sabouraud's Agar should
be used to confirm your diagnosis.

    Treatment of airsacculitis due to Aspergillus does not exist.
Potassium iodide therapy coupled with antibiotics and vitamin supplements will prolong the bird's life a few months, but it will eventually die. The dilemma you will face is how to diagnose airsacculitis.
Again, if you are fortunate enough to auscultate sounds of air sac
disease and associate them with the signs of poor condition and
dyspnea, you are on your way. In most cases, however, you can be
proud you were able to localize the problem to the respiratory system.
At any rate, the treatment for airsacculitis due to causes other than
Aspergillus involves the persistent use of antibiotics, vitamin
supplements, and a nonstressful environment. Even then advanced cases
will terminate.

    3. Air sac mites (Sternostoma and Cytodites) are found mainly in
canaries, finches, and parakeets. Their life cycle is unknown but it
is theorized that nestlings become infected by parents regurgitating
nutrients and mites. Signs include decline of physical condition,
respiratory distress, coughing, sneezing, and gasping, all of which
can be confused with Syngamus, Aspergillus, or pox infections. Often
times, the mites irritate the bird so much it cannot sleep. In reality, the only way you will diagnose air sac mites is to find them on
necropsy. So, you will have difficulty with isolated birds. In
aviaries, however, sacrificing one or two diseased birds for necropsy
is common practice.

    Several therapeutic regimes have been described for air sac mite
infestation. One involves mixing 0.05 gm of carbaryl in 1 ml of olive
oil and thoroughly dispersing in 50 gm of seed. Offer this treated
seed for 2-3 days every 2 weeks for three treatments. Another treatment uses 100 mg Neguvon per liter of drinking water for 3 ten-day
periods with a 20 day interval of nonmedicated drinking water given
between each 10 day period. Although Neguvon at 100 mg/liter water
is 90% efficacious, extreme care must be taken since the LD_{50} is only
200 mg/liter water. A third air sac mite treatment which is quite
primitive and very nearly borders on quackery is the placement of the
bird in a paper sack along with ¼ teaspoon of 0.5% carbaryl (Sevin
dust). Gently shake the bag to stir up the carbaryl which is inhaled.
Time in the bag should be 30 seconds. Do not put more than one bird
in the bag at a time and always use a modest amount of carbaryl.
Therapy should be repeated every 30 days until signs abate.

    Finally, pest strips make a good air sac mite preventative, pro-
vided the bird cannot get to them, and only if the bird is not held
within a small enclosure.

4. <u>Subcutaneous emphysema</u> occurs when one of the peripheral air sacs is torn or punctured, either from environmental trauma or from surgery. The lesions are quite spectacular, as a piece of tissue, muscle, fat, or subcutaneous fascia, acts as a valve letting air from the air sacs pass out under the skin but not back in. A large pocket of air or a diffuse subcutaneous emphysema forms. Treatment involves surgical repair and topical antibiotics to prevent infectious air-sacculitis. In repairing the torn air sac, never irrigate with saline or Ringer's lest the fluid make its way to the lungs and drown the bird.

LUNGS

Before discussing pneumonic conditions or pneumonias, a word should be said about congestion. More often than not, you will be localizing signs of respiratory disease to the lung on necropsy. Almost always, due to the fragility of the air capillaries, agonal congestion will be present in the lungs. Some clinicians claim to be able to distinguish passive congestion from active congestion or to recognize congestion with edema in the avian lung, but the authors do not believe it is possible. If you see lung congestion it is most likely agonal artifact. In the back of your mind, however, you should consider heart failure or partial obstruction of great vessels by a tumor or dysplastic thyroid as a cause of passive congestion.

Pneumonia, as with airsacculitis, is bacterial, viral, mycoplasmal, or fungal in origin. In general, true inflammation of the lung rarely occurs as a separate disease entity. It is usually related to an acute septicemia or is an extension of a disease process occurring in another system of the body. The exception is aspergillosis in which the inhalational route of entry permits an isolated pneumonic condition to develop.

The signs presented by a pneumonia are the same as those previously discussed as common respiratory signs, i.e., tail-bobbing, dyspnea, abnormal respiratory sounds, anorexia, ruffled feathers, etc. Since the pneumonia is often related to another diseased system or a septicemia, other signs will also be evident. Watery feces with renal involvement, edema and cyanosis if the bird is septic, or catarrhal exudate and sinusitis with an upper respiratory problem are all possibilities.

The bacterial causes of pneumonia include the agents of fowl cholera, <u>Pasteurella</u> <u>multocida</u>, <u>P</u>. <u>pseudotuberculosis</u>, <u>E</u>. <u>coli</u>, <u>Klebsiella</u>, <u>Erysipelothrix</u> <u>rhusiopathiae</u>, <u>Streptococcus</u> species, and <u>Salmonella</u> species. Cultures can be done on tracheal or sinus exudate antemortem or on the lung tissue itself postmortem. Antibiotic sensitivity should be determined at the same time to ensure that proper therapy is given (Table 6.2).

Gross lesions are often absent in acute conditions. Congestion and edema are present prior to death, but become obscured by agonal changes. In birds that live long enough, miliary necrotic foci are seen. Purulent exudate in small amounts may also be present.

TABLE 6.2. A Specific Therapeutic Regime for Infectious
            Respiratory Disease

1. Culture respiratory exudate--
    a. Use appropriately sized syringe with no needle; attempt
        to aspirate exudate from nares.
    b. Place exudate in transport media; brain heart infusion
        broth or tryptose phosphate broth.
    c. Streak on blood agar and isolate.
    d. Run an antibiotic sensitivity.
2. Place bird in 85-90°F heat for 30 days.
3. Hospitalize for first 7 days.
    a. Give Gentocin .00034-.0005 ml/mg IM, SID in the morning
        for 7 days (Schering-50 mg/ml).
    b. Nebulize 1 hour in the evening SID for 7 days using 4 ml
        of Gentocin in 15 ml of saline.
4. Give carbenicillin indanyl sodium (Geocillin from Roerig -
    500 mg tablet) while in hospital and for 10 days after dis-
    charging. Crush ½ tablet (or 250 mg) and mix with 4 oz H_2O.
    Use as sole source of drinking water.
5. Give vitamin ADE supplement for 30 days.

The principal viral infections are Newcastle disease and avian
pox. Newcastle disease, discussed in detail in Chapter 13, incites
a mononuclear inflammatory response in the trachea, bronchi, and lung
tissue. To confirm ND as the etiologic agent, virus isolation of lung
and trachea can be performed, or serology by hemagglutination, or
hemagglutination-inhibition conducted. Slaughter of infected birds is
required by law. Avian pox is mainly an upper respiratory problem
but does cause proliferative lung lesions in small birds. Stress-
precipitated mycoplasmal infections are suspected to occur, but few
reports and little research has been done to actually confirm it.

Finally, we will end our discussion of the respiratory system
with a review of a very common caged bird lung disease, aspergillosis.
Aspergillus fumigatus is ubiquitous and grows readily on any dead
vegetable matter. It is commonly seen wherever hygiene and living
conditions are poor or when antibiotics are used excessively or indis-
criminately. Again, diagnosis requires visualization of gross lesions
on necropsy or culture of tracheal exudate antemortem. Outbreaks of
"brooder pneumonia", common in domestic turkeys which inhale
Aspergillus spores in the incubator are rare in caged birds. The
route of infection then, is by inhalation of spores.

Aspergillosis is a chronic disease with variable signs. Birds
will appear quite healthy until respiratory distress and abnormal
respiratory sounds become evident right before death. Anorexia and
wasting are also seen near the end. The lung lesions are classically
described as pearls, or dense white cheesy masses. The lung tissue
consolidates focally or totally as a mycotic granulomatous inflammation takes over. As with young turkeys, always check the tracheal
bifurcation for evidence of an Aspergillus lesions which could have
built up and finally obstructed the tracheal lumen, asphyxiating the

bird. _Aspergillus_ may also be found in the brain where it causes a mycotic encephalitis.

As previously stated, therapy for aspergillosis only delays death. Infected birds should be destroyed before they spread the disease any further and the environment should be cleaned up as much as possible. If you must treat, potassium iodide ½ to 1 grain per pint of the drinking water (or by gavage give 2.5 ml/100 gm body weight of the stock KI solution) can be used, but amphotericin B at the rate of 0.75 mg/kg IV every other day for 3 days has also been used and is now the preferred treatment.

To summarize, we leave you with our scheme for diagnosing and treatment respiratory problems in caged birds. First, while the bird is alive, consider yourself lucky to have figured out that the bird is sick because of a respiratory disorder. A good physical exam and history may help you localize the problem further, but it is unlikely unless some cardinal sign, such as a swollen infraorbital sinus or a palpable thyroid, is very obvious. Frequently, a radiograph may provide a clue as the air density characteristic of the lungs and air sacs are partially or totally replaced by the water density of exudate and consolidation. The problem here is that radiology requires anesthesia, and birds with respiratory conditions are poor anesthetic risks. Treatment should be symptomatic, including a nonstressful environment, systemic antibiotics (Table 6.3); nebulization, a vitamin supplement and good nutrition. Forcefeeding may be required initially and the ambient temperature should be kept at 85°F for several weeks. Do not provide constant light or the bird will not sleep adequately.

Inhalation therapy or nebulization (Table 6.4) is a relatively recent mode of therapy in avian medicine. It is used almost exclusively for respiratory conditions. The technique involves placing a nebulizer inside an incubator with the bird, or if the bird is small, placing it inside a nebulizing jar. Treatment lasts 1 hour per day for 7-10 days.

The vehicle used in nebulization is sterile saline and the drug of choice (Table 6.3) is added to it. Atomization of this solution produces a fine mist which the bird tolerates very well. It should be done at room temperature since higher temperatures promote fungal growth. The two principal benefits of aerosol therapy are (1) the topical deposition of antibiotics onto the inflamed respiratory epithelium if the atomized particles of antibiotic/saline are the correct size (< 10 microns), and (2) humidification of affected respiratory epithelium which has a soothing effect, reducing inflammation. Nebulization using malathion for _Cnemidocoptes pilae_ and air sac mites has also been proven efficacious as has the use of decongestants.

If your diagnosis is based on a necropsy, as might be the case when dealing with an aviary, you will have a much better chance of localizing the problem and offering a more specific treatment.

TABLE 6.3. Respiratory Drugs

Antibiotics*	Route*	Strength	Mfg.	Vol. per gram body wt.	Vol. per 30 gm parakeet
Tetracycline (Achromycin)	IM	100 mg/ml	Lederle	.00034 ml BID	.01 ml
Chloramphenicol (Chlormycetin)**	IM	100 gm/ml	Park Davis	.00034-.0005 ml BID	.01 - .015 ml
Spectinomycin (Spectam)	IM	100 mg/ml	Abbott	.0013-.002 ml BID	.04-.06 ml
Gentamycin (Gentocin)	IM	50 mg/ml	Schering	.00034 ml BID	.01 ml
Tylocin** (Tylan)	IM	50 mg/ml	Corvel	.00034-.00068 BID ml	.01-.02 ml
Carbenicillin idanyl Na (Geocillin)	PO	500 mg tab	Roerig	Crush ½ tablet and mix in 4 oz H_2O. Use as drinking H_2O.	

* It is assumed that all birds with infectious respiratory disease will not drink. Therefore, antibiotics are initially given parenterally.
** Chloromycetin and tylocin offer the least tissue reaction.

OTHER USEFUL DRUGS IN THE RESPIRATORY SYSTEM

Expectorant
Potassium guaiacol sulfonate - 3 mg/oz of H_2O; give p.o. as needed.
Insect Bites
Dexamethasone - .0002 mg/gm IM SID until signs abate.
Trichomoniasis
Dimetridazole (Flagyl or Emtryl) - .05 mg/gm p.o. SID for 5 days; toxic to finches.
Candidiasis
Nystatin. Oral Suspension USP (Mycostatin from Squibb) - give amount equivalent to ¼ crop volume by gavage BID; place 2 drops in mouth.
Aspergillosis
Potassium iodide - 30-65 mg/pint of H_2O; give 2.5 ml/100 gm by gavage initially, then use stock as drinking H_2O.
Amphotericin B - 0.75 mg/kg IV every other day for 3 days.
Syngamus trachea - gapeworm
Thiabendazole - 50-200 mg/Kg SID p.o. for 7-10 days.
Air Sac Mites
1. Carbaryl (Sevin) - .5% dust; place ¼ teaspoon dust and bird in bag and thump with finger for 30 seconds. Repeat in 30 days, or nebulize with malathion.
2. Neguvon - 100 mg/liter drinking water for 3 ten-day periods with a 20 day interval of nonmediated water between each 10 day period.

TABLE 6.4. Nebulized Medications

Drug	Brand Name	Manufacturer	Strength	Dosage
Gentamycin	Gentocin	Schering	50 mg/ml	200 mg in 15 ml vehicle*
Spectinomycin	Spectam	Abbott	100 mg/ml	200 mg in 15 ml vehicle
Chloramphenicol succinate	Chlormycetin	Park Davis	100 mg/ml	200 mg in 15 ml vehicle
Kanamycin	Kantrim	Bristol	50 mg/ml	200 mg in 15 ml vehicle
Sulfadimethoxine	Bactrovet	Pitman-Moore	100 mg/ml	200 mg in 15 ml vehicle
Amphotericin B	Fungizone Intravenous	Squibb	50 mg/ml	100 mg in 15 ml vehicle

* A commercial nebulization vehicle is preferable although saline can be used.

QUESTIONS

1. What happens to exudate which forms in inflamed air sacs?
2. Name seven signs of respiratory disease in caged birds.
3. What is considered to be the cardinal sign of respiratory disease?
4. What are three conditions in caged birds which can be confused with respiratory disease?
5. How long does it take for a healthy, frightened bird to regain its normal respiratory rate?
6. Why do birds with respiratory involvement appear sleepy?
7. Where is the lesion in a bird which gapes or gasps and extends its neck in order to breathe? What could cause disease in this area?
8. A bird which occasionally coughs or sneezes and then swallows or gulps should be examined for what conditions?
9. What three conditions could cause dyspnea or explosive chirping on expiration?
10. What causes
    a. Serous rhinitis?
    b. Hyperkeratosis of the skin of the face and obstruction of the nares?
    c. Catarrhal rhinitis?
11. What is the therapy for an insect bite which is causing excessive swelling of the face of a caged bird and respiratory difficulty?
12. What is the treatment for sinusitis in parrots?
13. What two conditions frequently affect the oropharynx, larynx, and crop (ingluvius)? What is the treatment for each?
14. Name five conditions affecting the trachea of a pet bird and state a treatment for each.
15. What happens to fluid which accumulates in air sacs?
16. Does O_2/CO_2 exchange occur in air sacs?
17. What is the prognosis for <u>Aspergillus</u> infections of the lung and air sacs?
18. What do <u>Aspergillus</u> lesions look like?
19. What is the treatment for air sac mites?
20. What is the pathogenesis of subcutaneous emphysema occurring in a caged bird?
21. In most cases, treatment of pneumonia or other respiratory conditions is nonspecific and symptomatic. Describe this therapy.

CHAPTER 7

PROBLEMS OF THE DIGESTIVE SYSTEM

A. Introduction
B. Clinical Signs Seen with GI Problems
   1. Vomiting, diarrhea, and other signs
   2. Evaluation of droppings
C. The Mouth
   1. Avian pox
   2. Malocclusion due to deformed beak
   3. Vitamin A deficiency
   4. Candidiasis
   5. Trichomoniasis
D. The Crop
   1. Candidiasis and trichomoniasis
   2. Crop impaction
   3. Sour crop
   4. Regurgitation of crop contents
   5. Idiopathic necrosis of the crop
   6. Crop trauma
E. The Proventriculus and Gizzard
   1. Catarrhal inflammation of proventriculus
   2. Erosion of gizzard mucosa
   3. Atrophy of the gizzard muscularis mucosa
F. The Small and Large Intestines
   1. Stool examination and evaluation
   2. Five types of enteritis
      (a) Simple enteritis
      (b) Bacterial enteritis
         (1) Gram negatives are pathogens
         (2) Source of pathogenic bacteria
      (c) Hemorrhagic enteritis
      (d) Mycotic enteritis
      (e) Protozoal enteritis (Giardiasis)
   3. Cloaca - cloacal prolapse
   4. Constipation
   5. Coccidiosis

G. The Liver
    1. Hepatitis due to septicemia, toxemia, or other systemic
        conditions
    2. Pacheco's disease
    3. Fatty Liver
H. Helminth Parasitism of the GI Tract
    1. Roundworms
    2. Threadworms
    3. Proventricular and Gizzard Worms
    4. Tapeworms
    5. Thorny-headed Worms
    6. Flukes
I. Tables: 7.1. GI Signs in Birds and Their Causes
             7.2. Scheme for the Culture of Enteric Pathogens
             7.3. Therapeutic Regime for Bacterial Enteritis
             7.4. Therapeutic Regime for Hemorrhagic Enteritis

There are two basic ways to approach the study of GI problems in
pet birds. One would be an organ approach, reviewing the common
problems of each part of the alimentary canal: the other method is
the problem-oriented approach in which all the rule-outs for specific
signs or problems are considered. Because evaluation of digestive
disturbances in birds is more difficult than in mammals, we will com-
bine the two approaches by listing the few digestive problems you and
your client will see, and then proceeding with a full discussion of GI
problems on an organ basis, beginning with the mouth and ending with
the vent. The idea is for you to notice which digestive organs, when
diseased, cause the problems owners most often notice.

CLINICAL SIGNS SEEN WITH GI PROBLEMS
    As far as the client is concerned, there are only two main GI
problems, vomiting and diarrhea. The passing of undigested food in
the droppings, cloacal prolapse, and a pasted vent may be noticed by
a few watchful owners. All of these problems are clinical signs not
disease entities. As a veterinarian, you will observe the additional
signs of cheesy, catarrhal exudate in the mouth, distended crop, regurgitation, and perhaps constipation. Vomiting and diarrhea are by
far the most common signs reported. As we go through a systematic
discussion of the alimentary canal, pay special attention to which
diseases cause these signs (Table 7.1)

THE MOUTH
    The commonly seen conditions of the mouth are candidiasis, trich-
omoniasis, erosions due to vitamin A deficiency, caking of food under
the tongue, and pox lesions. Foreign body ingestion is not much of a
problem in caged birds as it is in gallinaceous birds.
    Pox lesions are focal erosions or ulcerations of the oral mem-
branes. They also may be distributed over the face, eyes, and legs.

TABLE 7.1. GI Signs in Birds and Their Causes

Problem	Causes
Vomiting (regurgitation)	Sour Crop Imitation courtship behavior Crop impaction Catarrhal proventriculitis Erosion of gizzard mucosa Candidiasis/trichomoniasis

Diarrhea	Parasitism
	Renal disease
	Abdominal tumor
	Psychogenic polydipsia
	Emotional stress
	Liver disease
	Enteritis (simple, bacterial, mycotic, protozoal, and hemorrhagic) precipitated by stress
	  - chilling
	  - drafts
	  - malnutrition
	  - change in ration
	  - spoiled ration
	  - fright
	  - physical injury
	  - change in routine

Passing whole, undigested seeds in stool	Intestinal hypermotility (enteritis) Atrophy of gizzard musculature No grit available to bird
Constipation	Dehydration Ingestion of excessive grit or fiber Obesity Inactivity Abdominal neoplasia Retained egg

Avian pox virus, as mentioned in other sections, is transmitted by insects. The condition is either self-limiting or lethal in caged birds. Your treatment should include removal of any crusts and administration of systemic antibiotics to prevent secondary bacterial infection. Commercial pox vaccines are not recommended, since they are intended for poultry and may be lethal to caged birds.

Birds with malocclusion due to deformed beaks frequently have food material trapped under the tongue. Soft food will form a plaque while whole seeds may migrate under the oral epithelium. Dysphagia, anorexia, and halitosis are the signs observed. Treatment consists of curretage and a beak trim. Another cause of malocclusion is beak rot. Apparently, Candida infects the region between the epithelium and horny tissue of the upper beak. The oral surface of the upper beak becomes necrotic, and because there is no hard tissue to oppose it, the lower beak grows abnormally. The prognosis for beak rot is very poor.

A thick, white, gray, or cream-colored epithelial membrane in the mouth, pharynx, larynx, or esophagus may be denuded oral mucosa caused by vitamin A deficiency. Another consideration should be exudate of a Candida or Trichomonas infection. Pigeons are especially prone to trichomoniasis. Budgies and canaries are also affected by trichomoniasis, with the lesions confined to the esophagus and crop. Candida and Trichomonas infections may occur in the mouth, oropharynx, and esophagus, but are usually an extension of a full-blown crop infection. A tenacious, cheesy to soapy, or catarrhal exudate over the mucosa is characteristic. Once you see this lesion you will never forget it. A stained smear of the exudate provides much diagnostic information. If Candida albicans is suspected, Sabouraud's agar may produce soft, creamy convex colonies containing oval-budding, yeast-like cells (use a lactophenol-cotton blue stain). Trichomonas gallinae, on the other hand, is a spherical or pear-shaped mastigophoran with an undulating membrane, 3-5 anterior flagella, and one posterior flagellum: a microscopic exam of the exudate is diagnostic. Trichomonas is usually transmitted to pigeon squab through regurgitated crop milk from the adult.

Candidiasis can be treated effectively with nystatin (Mycostatin Oral Suspension-Squibb) .25 ml per ounce body weight BID by gavage. Trichomoniasis is eliminated using dimetridazole (Flagyl or Emptryl), .05 mg/gm per oz SID for 5 days. One gram of nitrothiazole (Enheptin-American Cyanamid), dissolved in one liter of drinking water for 6 consecutive days, is also effective: this drug is toxic to finches, however. Control of trichomoniasis in a pigeon flock can be accomplished by periodic use of 1 ml of Nolvasan (Fort Dodge) in 1 quart of drinking water for 5 days.

THE CROP
We will describe six problems related to the crop: candidiasis/ trichomoniasis, crop impaction, sour crop, regurgitation of crop contents, idiopathic necrosis of the crop, and crop trauma.
1. Candidiasis and trichomoniasis have already been discussed. At this point we would like to emphasize the appearance of the gross lesions of these conditions in the crop. At necropsy, the normal crop wall will be thin and somewhat transparent. Candidiasis and trichomoniasis present a thickened, opaque crop wall whose mucosa looks like a turkish towel covered with cottage cheese.
2. Crop impaction occurs in obstructed seed-eating birds and birds which overeat grit after it has been withheld for some time. Old lesions of candidiasis may cause the mucosa of the crop/esophageal junction to swell and thicken, encroaching on the lumen and causing an obstruction. There may be other causes, such as neuromuscular disease, gastrointestinal inflammation, or greedy feeding in laying birds, but they have not been proven.

The basic sign is that of a bird with a large pendulous mass at the base of the neck. Palpation usually will identify this mass as the crop. It may be filled with a mass of dry material or it may contain abundant fluid. Using a little common sense, you can either turn the bird upside down and milk the ingesta out or you may proceed directly with the administration of a few drops of mineral oil, followed by gentle manipulation in an effort to break up the obstruction. If this conservative regimen fails, surgical intervention is required. Before you begin any therapy, attempt to rule out hyperplastic thyroids, fat deposits at the thoracic inlet, or tumor masses as the cause of the obstruction.

Old parakeets, it has been reported, will often have a slightly enlarged or pendulous crop. It has been postulated that old age or senility is the cause but there is no evidence to support this.

3. Sour crop is an inflamed or ulcerated crop containing foul-smelling, fermented ingesta. Regurgitation is frequently observed with this condition because the bird will flip crop material onto the top of his head and upper neck. The underlying mechanism of sour crop appears to be the development of a flaccid crop wall in which muscular tone and contractibility have decreased greatly. A mucoid fluid subsequently fills the crop. The cause of this flaccidity may be ingestion of spoiled, chilled, or moldy food, irregular feeding, any stress or infection which may disturb the normal function and transport capability of the alimentary canal caudal to the crop, or a primary inflammation of the crop itself, whether it be bacterial, fungal, or chemical in origin.

Therapy for sour crop involves milking out the crop contents two or three times a day followed by the administration by gavage of a tetracycline (Liquamycin Injectable-Pfizer), three drops two times daily (8 mg/day) for 7-10 days. Multiple vitamin supplements also may be added. Be sure to provide a complete and balanced diet. If this regimen fails, consistent use of kaopectate plus a very small amount of sodium bicarbonate may be administered by gavage. The idea is to coat the crop wall and reduce the acidity.

4. Neurotic regurgitation or imitation courtship feeding occurs commonly in healthy male parakeets. It is definitely a vice. These birds will attempt to feed anything shiny, especially their own image as seen through a mirror. Toys and even owners are the object of such behavior. Parrots occasionally will regurgitate to syrupy-talking owners (a response I find very appropriate and justifiable). This behavior is usually brought on by severe boredom. It can be easily cured in most cases by removing the object of the attempted feeding. Frequent environmental changes and the addition of a cage mate may be required. Medical treatment for this condition, especially if there is severe weight loss, involves the use of long-acting progesterones. Medroxyprogesterone acetate, 3 mg/100 gm IM, or megestrol acetate (dose by trial and error) are effective.

5. Idiopathic necrosis of the crop has been reported in parakeets housed in an outdoor aviary. The signs are a green slimy froth in the mouth and a green diarrhea. The cause is unknown and treatment is unproductive. The birds die within 20 days of the onset of signs.

6. <u>Crop trauma</u> results when a bird is left with no other choice but to stand and fight a cat. The bird will face the cat, flail its wings, reach out with its feet, squawk, and lose. The cat's claw or teeth usually lacerate the crop. Also, flying or homing pigeons attacked by hawks will show crop trauma. Surgical repair is required, demanding the suture line be very tight.

Iatrogenic penetration of the crop wall occurs from careless tube feeding of young cockatoos. In addition, crop surgery is frequently necessitated by a swallowed feeding tube which was bitten off by the bird as the tube was withdrawn from the crop. Having relaxed after feeding the bird, the holder will release the beak and jaw: the bird naturally closes its mouth, cutting the feeding tube.

THE PROVENTRICULUS AND GIZZARD

These organs are remarkably free of problems in caged birds. Debilitated, aged parrots may show catarrhal inflammation of the proventriculus or erosion of the gizzard mucosa, but these conditions can be diagnosed only at necropsy. Fungal involvement is common. Both of these conditions cause regurgitation and are treated nonspecifically by feeding an easily digestible diet and administering oral tetracycline.

Occasionally, atrophy of the gizzard muscularis mucosa is seen. The gizzard wall becomes extremely thin. This condition is manifested by cachexia and the passing of whole seeds in the droppings. The cause is unknown, but may be related to vitamin E/selenium deficiency.

Ingestion of a foreign body is rare. When it does occur, the foreign body may lodge anywhere in the upper alimentary canal, but the gizzard is usually as far as it goes. A radiograph is helpful in establishing a diagnosis if grit is not abundant. The bird may get along fine or show digestive upset or anorexia. Treatment involves surgical removal but the prognosis is very poor.

THE SMALL AND LARGE INTESTINE

The large intestine in birds is so short at the point where it joins the small intestine to the cloaca that we generally give it little emphasis with regard to the GI problems. Diseases of the small intestine, however, are very important. Diarrhea is the most common of all clinical signs seen in caged birds and is the primary indication of an enteritis.

As described in the section on examination of the cage, evaluation of the droppings provides considerable information. The normal dropping is half uric acid and half feces. A dropping which is predominantly white from uric acid is suggestive of renal disease. Bits of tissue or blood in the feces indicates there is a severe enteritis, while the passing of whole, undigested seeds suggests intestinal hypermotility or atrophy of the muscularis mucosa of the gizzard. A loose, unformed, off-colored stool, or a watery stool means diarrhea. Diarrhea, of course, is a clinical sign; enteritis is the disease entity associated with diarrhea. There are five types of enteritis in

caged birds: simple enteritis, bacterial enteritis, hemorrhagic
enteritis, mycotic enteritis and protozoal enteritis.

    1. Simple enteritis shows only diarrhea and no other signs. The
bird is active and alert. Simple enteritis is seen in isolated birds
which have experienced some type of stress. No infectious agents are
involved. The specific stress may be a change in ration, malnutrition, a spoiled ration, fright caused by a predator, a chill, a physical injury, or a disturbance of normal routine, such as not covering
the cage at night or opening a window which creates a draft. An emo-
tional disturbance, ingestion of paint, plaster, soap, or houseplants,
or nervous overconsumption of water (psychogenic polydipsia) are other
causes of simple enteritis. The pressure of an abdominal tumor on the
intestine or kidneys may also be an etiology. The primary treatment
for simple enteritis includes the removal of the inciting stress.
Administration of two drops of oral kaopectate three times a day for
2-3 days and the removal of all grit for 5 days are also recommended.
Five drops of paragoric in one ounce of drinking water may also be
tried. If the bird is expensive you should culture the feces without
hesitation.

    2. Bacterial enteritis or infectious enteritis may be a primary
intestinal problem or a manifestation of a systemic disease. Pathogenic bacteria are present in the gut in both instances and signs
other than diarrhea are also present. These signs include depression,
ruffled feathers, anorexia, polydipsia, and pasted vent. The stool is
soft, watery, unformed, and a variable color. Bacterial enteritis may
start out as a simple enteritis or it may result from an infection
with pathogenic bacteria coupled with some stress.

    A very critical point is that gram-negative bacteria are not
normal intestinal flora in seed- and nectar-eating birds. Any gram-
negative bacterium cultured from the dropping is considered a pathogen. The main source of enteric pathogens is fecal contamination of
water, food, perches, and cage floors. Fecal material in heated
aviaries is an excellent medium for bacterial growth. Another source
of infectious bacteria is a carrier bird which may itself become sick
if stressed. Nestlings are frequently infected by carrier parents and
exhibit diarrhea long before they ever eat material other than crop
milk.

    Another popular theory suggests that small numbers of gram-nega-
tive bacteria are in fact normal to the GI tract. Any factor which
affects peristalsis permits overgrowth of the gram-negative bacteria,
predisposing the bird to coliform enteritis. The real danger is that
a bacteremia and/or toxemia will occur, a definite life-threatening
condition.

    The most common enteric pathogens are E. coli, Salmonella,
Staphylococcus, and Pseudomonas. Other coliforms may also be cultured. Birds with Salmonella infection usually show severe depression
and shock. Bacterial enteritis is treated by performing a culture
and sensitivity test on the loose stool. Table 7.2 details a culture
scheme. In the meantime, parenteral and oral administration of broad-
spectrum antibiotics should be instituted. Fluids may also be considered. Table 7.3 outlines in-hospital and at-home therapeutic regimes.

TABLE 7.2.   Scheme for the Culture of Pathogenic Bacteria
from Bird Droppings*

1.   Aseptically place about 1 gm of a 24 hr fecal specimen in 4 or 5
ml of nutrient broth or BHI broth.   Mix well.

2.   Incubate at 35-37°C with loose cap for 4 hours.

3.   Streak one loopful on a blood agar and a MacConkey's agar plate.

4.   Incubate at 35-37°C for 24 hrs.   A preliminary readout is available in 12 hrs.

Interpretation

1.   Gram-negative and hemolytic gram-positive bacteria are not normal
intestinal flora in seed- and nectar-eating birds.   Therefore, no
growth on MacConkey's agar with growth, but no hemolysis, on a
blood agar plate is normal.   There are no pathogenic bacteria.

2.   Growth on a MacConkey's agar → Gram negatives present.

   a.   White or colorless colonies → Proteus, Salmonella, Arizona,
   Edwardsiella, Shigella, or Pseudomonas.   If Salmonella is
   suspected (severe depression or shock) enrichment media
   should be used since other bacteria usually overgrow salmonella on MacConkey's agar: Selenite broth → brilliant green
   agar → TSI slant.

   b.   Pink to brick red colonies → coliforms: E. coli, Klebsiella,
   Citrobacter, Aerobacter.

3.   No growth on MacConkey's, hemolysis on blood agar → staph or
strep.

4.   Growth on MacConkey's, and hemolysis on blood agar →

   a.   Hemolytic gram-negative bacteria, or

   b.   Hemolytic gram-positive and nonhemolytic gram-negative
   bacteria.

   *   "Fecal Monitoring of Caged Birds" by R. E. Dolphin, D.V.M. and
D. E. Olsen, D.V.M. in VM/SAC, June 1977: 1081-1085, with permission.

TABLE 7.3. Therapeutic Regime for Bacterial Enteritis

1. Perform a culture and sensitivity or go with a broad-spectrum
   antibiotic.
2. Mild enteritis can be treated at home with oral antibiotics.
3. Rehydrate the bird with lactated Ringer's solution if necessary.
   Fluids may be administered by subQ injection or gavage (see
   section on chemotheray).
4. The most ideal method of treatment consists of both parenteral and
   oral administration of antibiotics:
   a. For quick blood levels give IM injection for 1-3 days; oral
      antibiotics should be given by gavage simultaneously in
      severe cases in order to reduce the numbers of pathogenic
      bacteria in the gut.
   b. On subsequent days antibiotics can be given only by gavage
      with a protein and vitamin supplement.
   c. When the bird begins to eat and drink, place the antibiotics
      in drinking water.

ORAL MEDICATION
   * Gram-positive bacteria

Medication	Dosage	Convenient Measure
Tetracycline (Lederle)	350 mg/pt drink. H_2O	1 tsp/8 oz drink. H_2O
Lincomycin, 100 mg/ml (Upjohn)	200 " " " "	6 drops/oz " "
Tylosin, 50 mg/ml (Elanco)	200 " " " "	12 " " " " "
Erythromycin, 200 mg/ml (Abbott)	200 " " " "	3 " " " " "
Chloramphenicol, 100 mg/ml (Parke-Davis)	320 " " " "	6 " " " " "

   * Gram-negative bacteria

Chloramphenicol, 100 mg/ml (Parke-Davis)	320 mg/pt drink. H_2O	6 drops/oz drink. H_2O
Ampicillin, 200 mg/ml (Bristol)	125 " " " "	2 " " " " "
Kanamycin, 50 mg/ml (Bristol)	125 " " " "	8 " " " " "
Spectinomycin, 100 mg/ml (Abbott)	125 " " " "	4 " " " " "
Amoxicillin, 50 mg/ml (Beecham)	0.25 ml/oz body wt. twice daily	

Parenteral (IM) doses of these same drugs are given in the section on
chemotherapy. Use gentamycin judiciously if the bird is dehydrated or
toxicity will occur.

   * Drugs and dosages from "Antibiotic Therapy" by R. E. Dolphin,
D.V.M. and D. E. Olsen, D.V.M. in VM/SAC Sept. 1977: 1505, with
permission.

3. <u>Hemorrhagic enteritis</u> has an unknown etiology but it has been associated with the ingestion of table food, a spoiled ration, and liquor or beer. The stool is fluid, red with blood, and may contain bits of tissue. This condition can be fatal in 24-48 hours and should be considered an emergency. Treatment is mainly supportive. Provide a heated (85-90°F), nonstressful environment and offer no food for 24 hours. After this period only seed should be offered for about a week. Table 7.4 offers more specific therapy.

TABLE 7.4.   Therapeutic Regime for Hemorrhagic Enteritis

1. Provide a heated (85-90°), nonstressful environment.
2. Tetracycline, 25 mg/oz of drinking water for 4-7 days. If bird will not drink, fill the crop twice a day by gavage.
3. If dehydrated, give fluids.
   a. Subcutaneous injection of Lactated Ringer's (see Chemotherapy section for appropriate volumes).
   b. By gavage, deliver a solution which is ½ Lactated Ringer's and ½ dextrose (50%).
4. By gavage, give 3 drops of buttermilk to re-establish intestinal flora.
5. Give paragoric, 5 drops/oz of drinking water, for 3-4 days. If bird will not drink, give by gavage.
6. Offer bird a bland diet: buttermilk, crackers, and bananas.

4. <u>Mycotic enteritis</u> is an extension of a crop mycosis, usually candidiasis. It is quite rare. Common diarrhea is the presenting sign: other signs may or may not be present. Mycotic enteritis is usually discovered when small mucoid-fringed colonies instead of bacterial colonies are found on blood agar plates. Microscopic exam reveals the budding cells of <u>Candida</u>. Treatment with oral pediatric Mycostatin suspension (Squibb), two drops per 30 grams of bird, by gavage. Drinking water medication is not feasible since Mycostatin is a suspension and will precipitate out of solution. Control is accomplished with the disinfectant Nolvasan (Fort Dodge), one ml per quart of drinking water for 5 days.

5. <u>Protozoal enteritis</u>, although not widely reported, is common in aviary birds and is characterized by chronic or recurrent diarrhea. The etiologic agent is the flagellated intestinal protozoan <u>Giardia</u> of the family Hexamita. <u>Giardia's</u> habitat is the lumen of the small intestine. It also attaches to the villi in the mucosa. The active form, known as a trophozoite, has double nuclei, imparting a monkey-faced appearance to the organism. Division of these nuclei produces an inactive cyst with four nuclei which passes out of the bird in the feces. Transmission of <u>Giardia</u> is by ingestion of materials contaminated with feces containing the organism.

The chief sign of giardiasis is a foul-smelling, discolored mucoid stool. Depression, anorexia, weight loss, and ruffled feathers are also seen. Mortality is 20-50% if untreated. The condition occurs mainly in the warmer months and appears to be stress related. The weight loss and emaciation are caused by malassimilation due to malabsorption which creates steatorrhea, thus accounting for the soft putrid, amorphous stools.

Diagnosis of giardiasis is made by observing trophozoites in a fresh stool (detection of cysts is unreliable). However, a scraping of the intestinal mucosa in a sacrificed aviary bird or examination of the lumen contents provides the best results. Treatment with dimetridazole (Flagyl), 0.05 mg/gm p.o. SID for 5 days, is effective, although prolonged therapy may be required. Another brand of dimetridazole, Emtryl, is very effective at a concentration of 0.02% (1 teaspoon of Emtryl in a gallon of water) used as drinking water for 5 days. Halve the dose on hot days when water consumption is increased. This drug is toxic to finches, however. A good diet, excellent sanitation, and a nonstressful environment are also palliative.

CLOACA

Cloacal prolapse is caused by persistent diarrhea or the constant straining of a bird trying to pass a retained egg. The cloaca is often swollen, edematous, inflamed, and caked with cellular debris and fecal material. Our treatment consists of cleaning up the prolapsed portion of the cloaca, reducing the size of the swollen tissue, followed by manual reduction. Using mineral oil on a cotton swab, the debris is softened and removed. Granular sugar may then be applied for several minutes to shrink the tissue. After the sugar is removed, the cloaca can be anesthetized with cetacaine spray, saturated again with mineral oil, and reduced to its proper position with a glass thermometer. A purse string suture can then be placed around the margin of the vent and tied loosely enough to allow feces to pass. Some clinicians recommend using non-absorbable suture material which can be removed in one week. We have tried chromic gut, however, with good success. This absorbable suture material breaks down in 4-7 days, requiring no further capture and manipulation of the bird. The use of oily medication containing a local anesthetic, such as lidocaine hydrochloride ointment - 5%, a corticosteroid, and an antibiotic such as neomycin, in place of mineral oil alone has also been suggested. The diarrhea, of course, must be brought under control, or the bound egg extruded for this condition to remain resolved.

CONSTIPATION

Constipation in caged birds is rare. We do occasionally see it, however, in birds which are dehydrated. Other causes, such as ingestion of excessive fibrous material or grit, poor muscle tone due to inactivity or obesity, and pressure on the rectum due to a retained egg or abdominal neoplasm, have been described. Treatment involves removal of the inciting cause, administration of mineral oil by gavage, and warm soapy water enemas two or three times a day using an eye dropper or small, soft plastic tubing. Fruit and greens should be added to the diet.

Cloacal impaction with urates mimics constipation. Its cause is not known.

COCCIDIOSIS

In general, coccidiosis is not a problem in caged birds. It is occasionally seen in some passeriforms and is quite common in pigeons and gallinaceous birds. Antemortem diagnosis is accomplished by observing oocytes in a fecal flotation. Ten drops of a 16% solution of sulphamethazine per ounce of drinking water for three days, then a three-day period of no therapy, followed by another three days of treatment is effective in eliminating coccidiosis.

THE LIVER

It is next to impossible to diagnose liver disease in caged birds prior to death, unless SGPT and SAP measurements are made. Nonspecific signs include lethargy, anorexia, cachexia, diarrhea, obesity, seizures, blindness, polydipsia, and possibly abdominal swelling due to an enlarged liver and death. A radiograph can be very helpful. One report suggests liver disease can be diagnosed by observation of fecal urates which are colored an intense yellow-green instead of white.

Jaundice is extremely rare in caged birds. Liver disease is usually discovered at necropsy:

1. Hepatitis due to a septicemia, toxemia, or other systemic problem presents a dark, swollen congested liver. Hemorrhage or small focal bacterial granulomas may also be present. With time, acute hepatitis may be resolved by fibroblast invasion, creating a cirrhotic liver. In a psittacine showing airsacculitis, splenomegaly, and a swollen liver with rounded edges, psittacosis should be strongly suspected.

2. Pacheco's disease may appear as a diffuse necrotizing hepatitis with hemorrhage. Characteristic eosinophilic intranuclear inclusions in hepatocytes is pathognomonic for Pacheco's disease. Other viral hepatitis conditions may show focal necrosis, bile duct proliferation, and mononuclear cell infiltration. None of these lesions are specific for a virus infection.

3. Fatty liver occurs frequently, especially in parakeets showing the same nonspecific signs listed earlier. As in mammals, fatty change may occur as a result of nutritional, toxic, or infectious factors. The basic mechanism involves too much fat being presented to hepatocytes with a subsequent buildup of fat throughout the hepatic parenchyma. For instance, the liver of an overfed bird may not be able to handle the fat it receives when the bird is stressed, or an obese bird, when starved, may mobilize more fat than its hepatocytes can handle.

In another example, a common feed contaminant, aflatoxin, actually disrupts the cellular metabolic machinery rendering hepatocytes incapable of handling fats. Chronic aflatoxicosis leads to severe hepatic cirrhosis. Unproven treatment with lipotropic substance (Methiscol, .01 ml per 30 gm bird) plus B complex vitamins can be administered daily. A return to a complete and balanced diet in a nonstressful environment will also help. Massive doses of dexamethasone, 0.1 ml IV SID for 5 days for a 30 gm bird, have been reported successful in the treatment of aflatoxicosis.

If hepatitis is suspected antemortem, the only thing to do is cover the bird with a systemic antibiotic for 2-3 weeks and administer a multi-vitamin supplement. A heated, nonstressful environment and a good ration should be provided. Response to therapy is indicated when the bird shows increased vigor and its weight increases.

HELMINTHIC PARASITISM OF THE DIGESTIVE SYSTEM

Roundworms (Ascaridia spp)

Roundworms are quite common in cage and aviary birds, especially larger Australian parakeets and cockatiels. Canaries appear to be the only exception.

The life cycle of Ascardia spp is direct. Eggs are passed in the feces and require 2-3 weeks of development to reach the infective stage outside the host. Although direct sunlight will kill the eggs, under favorable conditions of warmth and dampness, eggs can remain viable for 3 months or more. After ingestion by the bird, larvae are released in the small intestine where maturation to the adult form occurs. Adults commonly measure 30-40 mm long.

Clinical signs of infection are variable. Emaciation, anorexia, growth retardation and diarrhea are commonly observed. Paralysis of the legs has been reported. Small numbers of worms may cause severe debilitation due to their large size and possible intestinal obstruction. Ascariasis is diagnosed by observation of adult worms or eggs in the feces using standard fecal flotation techniques.

Administration of 2 gm piperazine citrate per quart of drinking water daily for 3-4 days and repeated in 14 days is effective treatment. For birds that do not drink liberal amounts of water, such as the parakeet, a solution containing 50 mg piperazine/ml at a dose of 15 mg/30 gm bird can be given and repeated if necessary. Other effective treatments include thiabendazole in single oral doses of 20 mg/kg, or levamisole hydrochloride at 40 mg/kg, either orally or by intramuscular injection 14 days apart. It may be difficult for small birds to pass large numbers of roundworms, therefore administration of an intestinal lubricant would be helpful to eliminate the parasites.

In Australia, roundworms are countered with febendazole, 5 mg/100 gm bird. Levamisole HCl 2.5%, 0.1 ml/60 gm bird subcutaneously, is also used quite effectively. Dosing all birds every 6 weeks for 6 months is a chore, but it is the only way to rid an aviary of a roundworm problem. Since larval migration is a serious consequence of ascarid parasitism, antibiotics are always administered during the deworming treatment.

Good hygiene and sanitation is necessary for prevention and control of roundworms. Damp floors and beddings and leaky waterers are to be avoided.

Threadworms (Capillaria spp)

Capillaria spp or threadworms, may infect psittacines, pigeons and canaries. Threadworms are found primarily in the small intestine and occasionally in the crop or esophagus. Depending on species, the

life cycle is direct or indirect. Embryonated eggs can remain infective for many months.

Light infections are well tolerated. Birds with more severe infection may develop greenish to slimy-yellow, bloody diarrhea and exhibit emaciation, anorexia, and anemia. Fatalities are frequent,
especially among canaries.

Diagnosis is made by examining the droppings with standard fecal
flotation techniques. Characteristic thick-shelled, bipolar, plugged
oocytes measuring approximately 50 μ x 25 μ are diagnostic. At
necropsy adult worms measuring about 20 mm long are found adhering to
the intestinal mucosa. Treatment of choice is levamisole hydrochloride at a dose of 10-20 mg/kg either orally or by intramuscular injection.

Control measures involve good hygiene. Damp, warm cage floors
facilitate egg development. If treatment has been instituted, eggs
are no longer shed in the droppings after 48 hours. Therefore, birds
should be removed from contaminated cages 48 hours after treatment
to clean cages, and the old environment should be thoroughly disinfected.

Proventricular and Gizzard Worms

Proventricular and gizzard worms can infect a wide variety of
cage and aviary birds. The incidence of infection is low, however.
Adult worms are found primarily in the proventriculus but may perfor-
ate the proventriculus, resulting in peritonitis and air sac involvement. Habronema incertum is the most common species affecting cage
and aviary birds. The life cycle is indirect in all species, with
sow bugs, pill bugs, and cockroaches serving as intermediate hosts.

Affected birds may die from an acute attack, or if chronically
infected may exhibit emaciation and watery droppings containing mucus.
Diagnosis is based on identifying the eggs upon microscopic examination of the feces or by postmortem findings. Successful treatment
consists of using thiabendazole given at a single dose of 250-500
mg/lb body weight. Control is based on eliminating access to the
birds' surroundings by sow bugs, pill bugs, and cockroaches.

Tapeworms (Cestodes)

Tapeworms are found attached to the mucosa of the small intestine
in caged birds. These tapeworms are non-taenid cyclophyllideans, i.e.
the proglottids of the adult worms possess two genital pores and an
arthropod intermediate host (insect or mollusk) is required for completion of the life cycle. Therefore, grain and seed eaters are less
likely to become infected. Psittacine birds are primarily infected
by the genus Raillietina.

Clinical signs of tapeworm infection include general debility,
diarrhea, and loss of appetite and weight. Degree of pathogenicity is
not well correlated with the number of worms present.

Diagnosis is made by observing proglottids or eggs in the droppings. Treatment is generally unrewarding. Yomesan[R] has been used at
a single dose of 25 mg/kg body weight.

Control is aimed at eliminating the arthropod intermediate hosts, which are usually ants, beetles, or mollusks, depending on the species of tapeworm.

Thorny-Headed Worms (Acanthocephalids)

Acanthocephalids commonly affect passerines, raptors, and water fowl. The head or proboscis is laden with rows of hooks that attach to the intestinal mucosa.

The life cycle of acanthocephalids is indirect since arthropods are utilized as intermediate hosts. Annelids and other invertebrates may serve as carriers.

Heavy infections may produce anemia and debilitation. Inflammatory lesions may be found on the intestinal mucosa at the site of attachment.

Effective treatment is difficult, although thiabendazole at a single dose of 250-500 mg/lb body weight has been used.

Appropriate control measures are based on eliminating exposure to infective intermediate hosts and carriers.

Flukes (Trematodes)

Trematodes are dorso-ventrally flattened helminths that may parasitize virtually any part of the body, including the GI tract. Cage and aviary birds are unlikely to harbor flukes unless the birds have been recently captured or have access to pools of water containing snails. All bird flukes require mollusks for the development of immature forms and some flukes require a second intermediate host to become infective to their respective definitive host.

Proper sanitation of water sources will control infection.

QUESTIONS
1. Is coccidiosis a problem in caged birds?
2. What are the two most common GI signs reported by owners?
3. What are five conditions commonly affecting the mouth?
4. Which bird is most often afflicted with trichomoniasis? How do you treat this problem?
5. How do you recognize an impacted crop? What are the principal causes of this condition?
6. What is the cause of sour crop? What is the chief sign associated with it?
7. Why does a male parakeet regurgitate with no nestling to feed?
8. What conditions cause a bird to pass whole, undigested seeds in the feces?
9. What does excessive uric acid in the droppings indicate?
10. What types of enteritis occur in caged birds?
11. How do you recognize simple enteritis?
12. What stresses play a part in the development of enteritis?
13. Besides diarrhea, what signs are seen with a bacterial enteritis?

14. What is the main source of enteric pathogens?
15. Of what significance are gram-negative bacteria in the intestine of a bird?
16. How do you treat severe bacterial enteritis in a caged bird?
17. What causes cloacal prolapse in a caged bird? How do you treat it?
18. How do you diagnose liver diseases antemortem in caged birds?
19. What causes vomiting (regurgitation) in caged birds?
20. Briefly describe how you could perform a culture on the droppings of a bird.

CHAPTER 8

LAMENESS IN CAGED BIRDS

So many causes of lameness exist in caged birds that there is small correlation with the causes of lameness seen in mammals. The question Why is my bird crippled? is one you will be asked quite frequently. The etiologies of avian lameness are listed below.

Fractures or paralysis due to trauma
Use of perches of the wrong diameter
Cnemidocoptes pilae infestation of the legs and feet
Thread and tight identification bands
Compression of sciatic nerve or lumbosacral plexus by an abdominal tumor mass
Infectious arthritis secondary to trauma
Primary infectious arthritis
Bumblefoot
Rickets
Idiopathic dry gangrene
Nutritional deficiencies (other than rickets)
Plant and chemical toxicoses
Articular gout
Spraddle legs in young birds

Each of these etiologies will be discussed in detail, including a possible therapy for each.

1. <u>Fractures or paralysis due to trauma</u>. There are two main causes of trauma in caged birds. The first generally happens in the country of origin where very primitive methods of capture result in wing and leg fractures, missing toes, and occasionally damage to the CNS. Such trauma is common in larger psittacines where maneuverability and control during flight is limited. Not only is a bird captured from its natural habitat, but repeated captures also occur as it is transported by oceanic carrier to the port-of-entry quarantine station to the wholesaler to the retailer to the pet owner.

The second cause of trauma occurs when birds are allowed to fly freely indoors. Frequently a bird will become excited or frightened, or it may simply misjudge its flight pattern, causing it to slam head first into a wall. Brain trauma, paralysis, spinal fractures, and death often result.

91

If the bird is able to live with the lesion, whatever the cause of the trauma, it may one day be presented to you for diagnosis. Its gait, flight, attitude, or posture may be abnormal. Radiography will be very helpful in establishing a diagnosis but generally there is little you can do for these birds which were traumatized some time before presentation. Acutely traumatized birds can be treated by timely repair of fractures or the administration of antiedema doses of steroids for CNS trauma.

2. Use of perches of the wrong diameter. If a bird is forced to perch on a limb or pole of a diameter too large for that bird's foot, the foot pads will become sore and calloused and the feet will "break down," causing a severe lameness. Ideally, you should provide several perches, each a different diameter. The bird will select the perch that is best for him, but he will use all of them sometime during the day, providing excellent exercise for the feet and legs.

3. Infestation of the legs and feet with Cnemidocoptes pilae. The scaly leg and face mite burrows into unfeathered areas of the skin, feeding on keratin and stimulating an intense dermal inflammatory response with hyperkeratosis. The face, beak, legs, toes, and skin around the vent are the regions affected. If the mite infestation goes unchecked, thick, chalky, proliferative encrustations can form on the legs and toes, decreasing the range of motion and causing the bird to limp. Ankylosis of the hock and other joints can actually occur as the hyperkeratotic crusts overgrow the affected joint. A skin scraping is nearly always successfully diagnostic, revealing numerous sarcoptid mites. Treatment involves removal of the crusts after loosening with mineral oil. Subsequent applications of mineral oil will suffocate the mite, eliminating the cause of the inflammation.

4. Thin thread and tight leg bands. These two causes of crippled birds are so simple and obvious that they are often overlooked. Breeders and wholesalers may band a young bird's legs and forget to remove it. Or a free flying bird may get a piece of curtain thread wrapped tightly around its toe, leg, or wing. As the bird grows, the leg may increase in size or the band or thread may tighten for some other reason. The skin may actually overgrow this foreign material, making it difficult or impossible to see. Unilateral lameness is the usual sign. The bird may show considerable swelling, redness, or inflammation in the area, or there may be no reaction at all. Ultimately, circulation will become so impeded that the appendage will slough. Detection of the foreign body is accomplished by a close physical exam and radiography. Surgical removal is required in most cases.

5. Compression of sciatic nerve or lumbosacral plexus by a tumor mass. As mentioned in the section on neoplasia, the most common neoplasms seen in the abdomen of caged birds are ovarian adenocarcinomas, followed by embryonal nephromas. Each of these can exhibit uncontrolled growth and impinge on the lumbosacral plexus or the sciatic nerve. The affected limb will be weak and flaccid (lower motor neuron signs) and there will be an abdominal (sternal) lift which is a cardinal sign of a space-occupying mass in the abdomen. The prognosis is poor and

treatment of abdominal tumors in birds is not productive. Euthanasia
is recommended.

6. _Infectious arthritis secondary to trauma._ Weak, debilitated
birds are reluctant to move and often will rest on their breast and
hocks. Some poor flyers always land on their hocks. The repeated
trauma to the joint and tendon sheaths may result in a seropurulent
bacterial arthritis, usually _Staphylococcus_. Other bacteria can be
isolated, however. The joint should be tapped and a culture and
sensitivity test performed. Systemic antibiotic therapy is critical,
while intra-articular injection of an appropriate antibiotic and
dexamethasone to reduce inflammation are optional. Infectious arthritis as an extension of a septicemia also occurs. The etiologic agent
is usually _E. coli_, but _Pasteurella_, _Streptococcus_, and _Corynebacter-
ium_ have also been reported. Treatment is similar to that described
for traumatic staph arthritis.

7. _Bumblefoot._ Staphylococcal abscesses of the foot may be
unilateral or bilateral. Swollen foot and toe joints, severe pain,
and lameness are the signs. The staph infection produces a thick,
creamy, purulent exudate in the affected foot and toe joints and in
abscesses of the foot pads. Chronic bumblefoot shows a cheese-like
material or inspissated pus in these areas.

Poor management provides the predisposing factors to bumblefoot.
Use of course sand paper for cage floors, rough perches, hard concrete
aviary floors, and poor nutrition are usually seen. In cages infrequently cleaned, debris will stick to the toes and the bird will pick
at them, causing trauma. Also, sick or debilitated birds spend more
time on the floor where any scratch or abrasion on the foot pad can be
invaded by the ubiquitous staph organism.

Treatment of bumblefoot is very tricky because the bird has to
use the affected foot during your therapy. First, cover the bird
systemically with tetracycline or chloramphenicol. Then incise the
joint or foot pad abscess, flush with saline, currette, and pack with
an appropriate antibiotic and a proteolytic enzyme such as Elase^R,
an ointment containing deoxyribonuclease and fibrinolysin. Be sure
to perform a culture and sensitivity test in case you have a resistant
staph or some other pathogen. Bandage and place an Elizabethan collar
on the bird. Aggressive follow-up therapy is required if you are to
be successful and, of course, you should correct any mismanagement.

8. _Leg weakness and metabolic fractures due to rickets._ If
calcium or vitamin D_3 are deficient in the diet of birds, rickets will
develop. This condition is discussed in detail in the section entitl-
ed Nutritional Deficiencies. Briefly, vitamin D_3 or cholecalciferol
is produced in the skin by the conversion of its precursor, 7-dehydro-
cholesterol. Ultraviolet light from the sun effects this conversion.
Birds produce little vitamin D_3 in this manner because most are housed
indoors, receiving little sunlight, and because most of the skin is
feathered. Therefore, a majority of vitamin D_3 must be supplied in
the diet.

With a vitamin D_3 deficiency, calcium-binding protein cannot be
synthesized in the intestinal wall and absorption of dietary calcium
is impossible. Of course, if inadequate calcium is presented in the

diet, no amount of vitamin D_3 will prevent the signs of rickets. Bilateral leg weakness, soft pliable bones, a curved keel bone, knobby ribs, and a characteristic penguin-like squat are seen. Metabolic features are seen in advanced cases.

Therapy involves calcium and/or vitamin D_3 supplementation in the diet.

9. Idiopathic dry gangrene. Necrosis and sloughing of digits, toes, feet, wings, the tail, and focal areas of skin on the breast are commonly seen in parakeets with idiopathic dry gangrene. Attempts have been made to recreate this condition by feeding ergot but they have not been successful. In cases presented to us, we have been unable to grow any mycotic organism or detect any mycotoxin in the feed of the patient, and bacterial cultures were negative. As a result, this crippling condition has been labeled idiopathic dry gangrene. The condition is usually self-limiting; that is, the bird either dies or the gangrene remains localized. Many birds can actually live a functional life on the stumps that are left after sloughing. Treatment is debatable. Amputation proximal to the necrosis will produce a stumped, crippled bird, much the same result as with the condition itself. And topical antibiotics and steroids are little help in halting the necrosis, although secondary bacterial infections probably are prevented.

10. Nutritional deficiencies (other than calcium and vitamin D_3). The lack of certain vitamins will create either microscopic or gross lesions in the central nervous system, producing death or permanent nervous signs. Birds with paresis, paralysis, incoordination, or ataxia are reported by the lay person as being crippled. Lack of the following vitamins will present various signs related to the nervous system.

Vitamin B_1 (thiamine)--ataxia, paralysis, opisthotonus
Vitamin B_2 (riboflavin)--curling of toes, the lesion is a neuritis of the peripheral nerve
Nicotinamide--tremors, paresis
Vitamin B_6 (pyridoxine)--spastic clonic/tonic movements
Folic acid--paralysis with neck extended; tremors of wings flaccid
Vitamin B_{12} (cyanocobalamin)--no signs but neuronal degeneration occurs histologically
Vitamin E/Selenium deficiency--ataxia and paralysis in young parakeets due to encephalomalacia. Adult birds may show muscle weakness due to myopathy.

In most cases these avitaminosis conditions of the nervous system are incurable; the bird dies because it cannot feed or drink. A few birds, if treated early, will stop developing further nervous lesions and learn to live with existing lesions, while other cases will experience a total regression of signs and do quite well. Treatment mainly involves large doses of thiamine, although all of the vitamins of the B complex group should be administered, with a response expected in 24-48 hours.

11. Plant and chemical toxicoses. It would be safe to say that any household chemical would be toxic to a pet bird, but this is

particularly true of carbamate and organophosphate derivatives. They
usually bring quick death, but in minute, cumulative doses nervous
signs may be seen. Houseplants present a similar problem, compounded
by the bird's desire to munch on greenery. Examples of toxic plants
a bird might be exposed to are wisteria, rosary peas, boxwood,
azaleas, juniper, privet, evergreens, apple, cherry, peach, and euca-
lyptus trees, and eggplant, to name a few. The signs are variable,
but are usually nervous or gastrointestinal in nature. A big problem
is that we really don't know which plants are toxic to which species
of avian. Often we learn the hard way.

13. <u>Articular gout</u>. This metabolic disorder and the complex
therapy for it is fully discussed in the section on gout. For the
purpose of this chapter, it is enough to know that uric acid and urate
crystals are deposited in joint cavities, in adjacent connective
tissue, and in tendon sheaths, appearing as small, round, whitish-
yellow concretions in the skin, legs, and feet. To the untrained eye
these lesions appear to be small multiple abscesses. A diagnosis can
be made very easily by taking a biopsy and looking through a micro-
scope for urate crystals.

The main joints involved are the hock and foot joints. Birds
suffering from articular gout are restless and shift their weight
from one leg to another. Perching is difficult. Eventually the toes
and legs swell up and become very tender and painful. The prognosis
for gout is poor and treatment is unproductive but should be attempted
for isolated pet birds.

13. <u>"Spraddle legs" in young birds</u>. Spraddle or splay legs can
occur congenitally or may be induced by poor management. Without
rough nesting material in the form of sticks or twigs, birds such as
nestling pigeons (squab) and nestling doves are predisposed to spraddle legs. These birds will rest on their abdomen or breast and
flounder about when attempting to ambulate. Similarly, gallinaceous
birds must never be brooded on slick surfaces such as those covered
by newspapers. Sawdust or wood shavings are optimum. Otherwise,
spraddle legs may develop. One clinician reports increased calcium in
the diet of parents and nestling seems to be a preventative.

In all of these cases, the appendages are not supported properly
by the nest or brood floor, causing some slight rotation of the hock
joint which permits the gastrocnemius tendon to slip laterally. The
damage is permanent. One reason birds are unable to adjust very well
to poor floor conditions is that the adductor muscles of the leg are
very small and nearly nonfunctional.

From the preceeding discussion you can see that the reasons birds
show lameness are many. Undoubtedly there are other causes. Those
listed are the ones we frequently see clinically. A good history,
especially information about diet and environment, will provide you
the answer in many cases. Couple the history with a thorough physical
exam and the diagnosis will come easily.

QUESTIONS

1. Which vitamin deficiencies are manifested by nervous signs?
2. Why is vitamin D_3 needed for calcium absorption?
3. What are the signs seen in rickets?
4. Why are most birds unable to synthesize vitamin D_3 in their skin?
5. What comprises the skin and articular deposits seen in gout?
6. What is the prognosis for birds with gout?
7. What is bumblefoot? Describe the treatment for bumblefoot.
8. Intense hyperkeratosis on the feet and legs can cause lameness. What is the usual cause of this lesion in parakeets?
9. Of what significance is perch diameter?
10. Birds allowed to fly freely in the house can develop lameness for two reasons. What are they?
11. What factors predispose to spraddle legs?
12. What pathogen is usually found in purulent arthritis secondary to trauma?
13. If you see leg lameness and an abdominal lift what is the probable cause of the lameness?
14. Describe idiopathic dry gangrene in pet birds?
15. Why do so many imported parrots have bone fractures or missing toes?

CHAPTER 9

MAJOR NUTRITIONAL DEFICIENCIES AND METABOLIC PROBLEMS—RICKETS, GOITER AND GOUT

There are many disease conditions in caged birds which are caused by nutritional deficiencies or metabolic disorders. Vitamin B and Vitamin E/Selenium deficiencies are examples and they are discussed in the section on caged bird lameness. This chapter will deal with three very prevalent problems in pet birds: rickets, thyroid hyperplasia (goiter), and gout.

RICKETS

Rickets is a disease characterized by failure in adequate deposition of calcium (mainly calcium phosphate) in the bones of growing birds. Adult rickets is a term used to describe the essentially similar condition, osteomalacia, seen in older birds. There are three causes of rickets in caged birds:

1. Deficiency of dietary calcium. Obviously, if the bird is metabolically normal but is not presented adequate calcium in the diet, calcium cannot be deposited in bone. This is a a common cause of rickets when birds are not provided with a cuttle bone or oyster shell grit.

2. Deficiency of vitamin D_3. There are a number of chemically distinct forms of vitamin D, but only one form--vitamin D_3 or cholecalciferol--will act as the nutritional precursor of the hormone 1,25-dihydroxycholecalciferol, which is effective in promoting calcium absorption in the gut (Fig. 9.1). Cholecalciferol (Vit D_3) is produced by irradiation of 7-dehydrocholesterol (provit D_3) with ultraviolet light from the sun or an artificial source. This synthesis occurs in the outer skin layers. The 7-dehydrocholesterol is synthesized from abundant cholesterol in the body and deposited in the skin.

The cholecalciferol, or vitamin D_3, is transferred to the liver where it is hydroxylated to 25-OH-cholecalciferol or 25-OH-D_3. This compound is then transported to the kidney where further hydroxylation yields the hormone 1,25-$(OH)_2$-D_3, which is required for the synthesis of a specific calcium-binding protein in the intestinal wall. None of the forms of vitamin D participate directly in the absorption of calcium from the gut.

97

UV light

1.	Skin	Body cholesterol	$\rightarrow$ cholecalciferol (vit D_3)
2.	Liver	Vit D_3	$\rightarrow$ 25-OH-Vit D_3
3.	Kidney	25-OH-Vit D_3	$\rightarrow$ 1,25-$(OH)_2$-D_3
4.	Intestine	1,25-$(OH)_2$-D_3	

Substrate Calcium binding protein
(CaBP)

Calcium from
gut lumen $\downarrow$

5.	Blood	Ca
		$\cdot$
		Ca$\cdot$CaBP$\cdot$Ca
		$\cdot$
		Ca

FIG. 9.1. The synthesis and role of vitamin D_3.

The problem with caged birds is that most are housed indoors and do not receive enough direct sunlight to effect conversion of provitamin D_3 to vitamin D_3. As a result, 1,25-$(OH)_2$-D_3 cannot be produced, leaving the bird short on calcium-binding protein.

   3. A severely unbalanced calcium/phosphorus ratio. The normal calcium/phosphorus ratio is 1.5-2.5 to 1. Very simply, too much calcium will tie up phosphate ions in the gut lumen and be excreted as $Ca_3(PO_4)_2$. Since the phosphate ion is required for deposition of calcium in bone (as calcium phosphate), its depletion prevents mineralization. On the other hand, if there is too much phosphorus (PO_4^{-3}) calcium will be bound and excreted as $Ca_3(PO_4)_2$ and never make it across the gut wall. The lesson here is that a dietary calcium deficiency should not be corrected by preparing a diet containing excessive calcium. In most cases, crushed oyster shells offered free choice is palliative, since the bird will consume what it needs.

   Whether the cause of rickets is a dietary deficiency of calcium, vitamin D_3, or a severely imbalanced calcium/phosphorus ratio, the common denominator is a lowered blood calcium sometime during the disease. With time the parathyroid will turn on to produce more parathyroid hormone (parathormone or PTH) which will mobilize calcium from bone, eventually returning blood calcium levels to normal at the expense of the bone. Rickets then is nearly always accompanied by nutritional secondary hyperparathyroidism. We bring this point up because the parathyroids are normally too small to observe during the postmortem exam. A rachitic bird, however, will have hyperplastic parathyroids which appear as tiny dark dots on the caudal pole of the thyroids, which themselves are very small, So, if you can see the parathyroids, be suspicious of rickets and closely examine the skeletal system.

   The major sign of rickets in young birds is a severe weakness of the legs. This lameness is not noticed until the bird leaves the nest and attempts to walk. The beak and claws may be pliable, and with time the long bones of the legs may bow and the keel bone (sternum) may take on an S-shaped appearance. Knobby ribs which curve inward and spinal column deformities are also seen. In advanced cases metabolic fractures will occur. As a matter of fact, in performing a physical exam your palpation may produce a fracture, so be careful.

Leg weakness causes the bird to walk with obvious effort and rest frequently on its hocks. Feathering is poor and soft-shelled eggs are common in hens.

Often times a bird will be presented for necropsy so that you can provide the owner with the cause of death. Visible parathyroids, deformed, soft bones, and long bones which break easily when manipulated should lead you to a diagnosis of rickets.

Therapy for birds which you diagnose as rachitic should include calcium and vitamin D_3 supplements. A cuttlebone or crushed oyster shells will provide adequate calcium. Vionate[R], a multi-vitamin supplement from Squibb, is a good source of vitamin D_3, as is cod liver oil. Unfortunately, by the time rachitic signs are seen, the damage done is irreversible. Treatment cannot hurt, however, so give it a try.

THYROID HYPERPLASIA (GOITER)

Under normal conditions thyroxin, the active secretion of the thyroid, inhibits the release of thyroid-stimulating hormone (TSH) from the anterior pituitary. With this lower level of TSH the follicular cells of thyroid become quiescent, thereby preventing excessive production of thyroxin. Diets deficient in iodine, a substrate necessary for elaboration of thyroxin, upset this feedback system.

Decreased thyroxin due to iodine deficiency permits uncontrolled release of TSH by the pituitary and, in turn, increased levels of TSH cause thyroid follicular cells to proliferate in a futile attempt to produce adequate levels of thyroxin. The end result is a greatly enlarged, hyperplastic thyroid (goiter) containing little or no colloid. It is important to realize that thyroid hyperplasia does not mean hyperthyroidism, since the thyroxin levels are reduced.

The significance of goiter is two-fold. Lowered thyroxin levels decrease metabolic rate. The bird becomes lethargic and cannot cope with changes in ambient temperature. Also, fertility is reduced greatly. The major effect, however, is mechanical. As the thyroids enlarge they impinge on the trachea and syrinx, causing wheezing and labored breathing, signs most clients associate with respiratory disease. Chronic thyroid enlargement may even block the alimentary canal, leading to regurgitation or pendulous crop. In any case, debilitation and mortality eventually occur if therapy is not initiated.

As mentioned, the bird with goiter will be lethargic, preferring to perch in a crouched position with feathers ruffled. A clicking sound and faint wheezing with respiratory distress may also be noticed. The owner will firmly believe his bird has pneumonia.

Gross findings during a postmortem exam include enlarged thyroids. Normal thyroid glands in a parakeet measure 0.5 mm x 1-2 mm and are easily missed. Hyperplastic thyroids may be enlarged 5-10 times above normal and may be a brown-red color instead of tan. These enlarged thyroids, located on either side of the trachea in close proximity to the common carotid arteries and just anterior to the syrinx, are easily visible.

On histopathologic exam, the normal architecture of the thyroid is disrupted. Colloid is absent, the interstitial tissue between follicles is thickened, and the follicular epithelium is hyperplastic, forming complicated folds of epithelial cells into the small, shrunken follicles. A normal thyroid presents flat follicular epithelum surrounding variable-sized follicles distended with abundant colloid.

Therapeutic measures can bring relief if the goiter is not too advanced. Our treatment uses a solution of 1 ml of 7% Lugol's iodine in 14 ml of water. One ml of this diluted iodine solution is placed in each ounce of drinking water every day for 2 weeks. Lugol's solution (7%) contains the following ingredients:

Iodine crystals . . . .   6.0 gm
Potassium iodide . . . .   1.0 gm
Distilled water . . . . 100.0 ml

Dissolve the potassium iodide in the water. The iodide crystals will then go into solution readily.

Since surveys have shown that a majority of pet birds suffer from some degree of thyroid hyperplasia, owing to a seed diet containing inadequate iodine, we believe prophylactic supplements of iodine are essential. Finely ground oyster shell grit or cod liver oil provide high amounts of iodine. The cod liver oil, however, should be used judiciously since it contains so much iodine. A once-a-week dose of the diluted iodine preparation - one drop per ounce of water - is also effective.

Rations containing crushed soybeans (uncooked) or soybean meal should be avoided since they are goitrogenic. Apparently they inhibit iodination of thyroglobulin by the thyroid follicular cells, halting the formation of thyroxin.

GOUT

Gout is a poorly understood condition in which crystals of uric acid or urates are deposited in the tissues. In birds uric acid is the end product of protein catabolism, chiefly the purines (adenine, guanine, and xanthine). The conversion of xanthine to uric acid is catalyzed by the enzyme xanthine oxidase (Fig. 9.2). This synthesis occurs in the liver and kidney while elimination of uric acid occurs only via the kidneys. Among caged birds gout occurs frequently in psittacine birds and is quite rare in passerines.

The exact cause of gout is unknown. Several predisposing factors, however, have been identified:

1. _Increased amounts of uric acid presented to the kidneys_. In the face of a _high protein diet_ or just simply overeating, a normal liver and kidney may synthesize so much uric acid that the kidney is unable to eliminate it. Subsequently, blood levels of uric acid increase and exceed the limit of solubility, at which time precipitation in tissues occurs. A key element in this high protein diet

Adenine Guanine Hypoxanthine	xanthine oxidase $\rightarrow$	xanthine	xanthine oxidase $\rightarrow$	uric acid

FIG. 9.2. Purine metabolism in birds.

theory is inactivity. Inactive birds or birds confined to small cages and unable to fly do not have good muscular activity to stimulate circulation and thirst. With decreased water intake, hydration and diuresis is reduced, predisposing the bird to uric acid retention.

2. Impaired renal function. It has been theorized, due to a wide range of causes, that impaired renal function makes a bird susceptible to gout. Exposure to cold and dampness, intoxications, vitamin A deficiency, poor nutrition, and infectious diseases, all may interfere with renal function so that even though normal amounts of uric acid are presented to the kidney, its reduced capacity for excretion permits increased levels of uric acid in the blood and subsequent deposition of the acid or its salt into the tissues. Of particular interest is the hypothesis that a poor diet (one low in quality protein and vitamins but high in carbohydrates) will cause gout. The idea here is that the cellular mechanisms in the kidney are impaired by dietary deficiencies, resulting in nephrosis and gout. So diets high in protein and diets low in protein may predispose the bird to gout.

We do not want to leave you with the impression that renal disease causes gout, because we do not have adequate proof at this time. We know for certain that renal disease can occur without associated gout and that gout can occur without renal disease. In other words, we don't know whether renal disease is a consequence of gout or the cause of it.

There are two forms of gout, depending on the site of uric acid/urate crystal deposition: articular or synovial gout and visceral gout. It is generally agreed that articular gout is the chronic form and is more common than visceral gout, the acute form. A third form of gout, the renal form, has been postulated since necropsies frequently reveal urate crystals only in renal tissue. The question is whether or not the urate crystals are deposited in the renal parenchyma after death.

In articular gout, urates are deposited around the joints, ligaments, tendons, and tendon sheaths. Accumulations of these deposits appear as cream-colored, shiny swellings which bulge up through the subcutaneous and skin tissues. They are extremely painful, especially if the limb is manipulated, and they may disfigure the leg. The condition affects mainly the hock and joints of the feet and the tendon sheaths of the forearm; the hip and shoulder are never involved. If the urate concretion is incised, the deposit is found to be of a creamy, pasty, or gritty consistency, depending on how much fluid is present. It can be easily mistaken for an abscess. Simple microscopic exam will show needle-shaped or amorphous masses (tophi), or the murexide test can be used. A small amount of material from the tophus is placed on a slide and mixed with a drop of nitric acid. Using a bunsen burner, very slowly evaporate any moisture and allow to cool. Add one drop of ammonia. A red-purple color is positive for uric acid.

The signs of articular gout are those of a restless bird with a shifting leg lameness. The bird will seek out the largest perches or ones that are closest to the floor; it may even prefer the floor. The toes and legs become swollen, warm, and tender until the pain becomes so great that the bird refuses to move. If there are tophi in the wings, flight will not be attempted. It is remarkable that some birds do remain unaffected despite obvious lesions. Most, however, succumb to malnutrition.

Visceral gout is more insidious than articular gout and certainly more difficult to detect. It is probably less painful. Beige, white, pale yellow, or gray urate depositions are seen on the peritoneal or serous surfaces of any abdominal organ, but most frequently the liver, kidney, pericardium, heart, and air sacs. Visceral gout shows no diagnostic signs. Instead, the nonspecific signs of anorexia, emaciation, change in temperament, variable stool consistency, and lethargy are observed. The bird will suddenly appear dead on the cage floor. Often, however, visceral and articular gout are seen together and the diagnosis is no problem.

The prognosis for a bird affected with any form of gout is extremely poor. Your efforts will only prolong the life of the bird by several months. The problem is that although the therapy will prevent further urate deposition, it does nothing about the urates already embedded in the tissues of the body. Furthermore, the therapy is often arduous, requiring a consistent effort over a long period, something most owners will not sustain. Despite the poor prognosis, give therapy a chance (if the client is willing). Just be sure not to offer too much optimism.

Treatment of gout involves dietary and environmental management, administration of systemic drugs, and local treatment of subcutaneous urate deposits. Before regulating the diet you must establish whether the current ration contains high or low protein. A high protein ration can be modified by changing to a diet containing cereal products. On the other hand, protein can be increased by adding cooked egg, grubs, and insects. Most birds fail to respond to dietary changes, however, probably because the kidneys are already permanently damaged by the time therapy is initiated. Dietary management then is a helpful adjunct to the mainstay of gout treatment, the oral administration of allopurinol (Zyloprim[R] from Burroughs Wellcome).

Allopurinol is a structural analogue of hypoxanthine. Allopurinol and hypoxanthine compete for oxidation by the enzyme xanthine oxidase (Fig. 9.2). The main pharmacologic effect of allopurinol, however, is the direct inhibition of xanthine oxidase. Between inhibition of xanthine oxidase and the competition with hypoxanthine, allopurinol reduces the amount of uric acid formed by the liver and kidney, lowering the uric acid concentration in plasma below its limit of solubility and eliminating the possibility of precipitation of crystals into the tissues. The unoxidized xanthine and hypoxanthine are eliminated via the kidneys.

The problem with allopurinol therapy is that it does nothing to remove existing uric acid tophi already in the tissues. Their presence and the inflammatory response and pain they incite generally kill the bird within months, despite the therapy. Moreover, allopurinol must be administered daily for the rest of the bird's life.

Local treatment of articular gout may be warranted if the urate deposit on a foot pad or joint is causing great pain, swelling, and inflammation. Surgical removal and cauterization with silver nitrate is preferred, but the wound heals very poorly.

Nonstressful management will do much to enable the bird to tolerate the gout problem. Perches should be smooth and broad, made of soft wood, and placed at a low level since climbing is difficult. Food and water dishes should be easily accessible.

QUESTIONS

Rickets
1. What is rickets?
2. What age bird usually shows signs of rickets?
3. What are the signs and gross lesions of rickets?
4. What are 3 fundamental causes of rickets?
5. What is the optimum calcium/phosphorus ratio for caged birds?
6. How does a bird make vitamin D_3? Where is it synthesized?
7. What role does vitamin D_3 play in calcium absorption from the gut?
8. Why does a bird need an exogenous source of vitamin D_3?
9. What happens to the parathyroid glands in a rachitic bird? Why?
10. What is the therapy for rickets?

Thyroid Hyperplasia (Goiter)
1. Where are the thyroid glands located in a pet bird?
2. What size in millimeters are normal thyroids?
3. Describe the pituitary-thyroid feedback system.
4. What causes thyroid hyperplasia (goiter) in caged birds?
5. Why do the thyroid follicular cells proliferate?
6. What are the signs of goiter in caged birds?
7. What is the therapy for goiter?
8. What prophylactic measures can be taken?
9. What feedstuffs are goitrogenic?
10. Does thyroid hyperplasia mean hyperthyroidism? Why?

Gout
1. What is gout?
2. What are the two forms of gout seen in caged birds?
3. What is the cause of gout?
4. What factors predispose a bird to gout?

5. How does activity help reduce the possibility of gout occurring?
6. What enzyme oxidizes purines to uric acid?
7. What are the signs and gross lesions seen in:
    a. Articular gout?
    b. Visceral gout?
8. What is the prognosis for a bird with gout?
9. How does allopurinol work?
10. What are two reasons why allopurinol does not cure a bird with gout?

CHAPTER 10

TUMORS AND EGG-BINDING

Neoplasms are more common in the budgerigar than in any other vertebrate animal. A study by Beach in 1962 suggested that tumors were the cause of death in 25% of the parakeets he surveyed. Other researchers have estimated that 15% of all parakeets are afflicted by various neoplastic conditions, a frequency unparalleled among other birds and mammals. Of the 26 orders of the Aves class, the order Psittaciformes has the highest incidence of neoplasia, while the order Passeriformes has the lowest incidence. The reason for so much neoplasia within one group is unknown, although hereditary factors have been postulated.

In general, the ratio of malignant to benign neoplasms in birds is 2:1. Of the malignant type, 33% affect the skin and subcutaneous tissues, 33% involve the kidney, 15% are gonadal tumors, and 7% involve the blood, spleen, and the lymphatics. Bone and liver neoplasms make up less than 2% of the malignant types. On the other hand, 90% of the benign tumors involve the skin, mainly as lipomas, xanthomas, and papillomas.

Our clinical approach to tumors in caged birds is very simple. Neoplasms are placed in one of three categories based on the location in the body, and each category has a different prognosis and treatment. The three categories, although artificial, are as follows:
1. Tumors of the skin and subcutaneous tissues (skin).
2. Tumors of organs in the abdominal cavity (abdominal).
3. Tumors of the skeletal system (bone).

SKIN TUMORS

The main thing to remember about skin tumors is that a treatment does exist. Surgical excision, whether the tumor is benign or malignant, is preferred in pet birds for several reasons. First, the risks of performing a biopsy are as great as the risks of going ahead and removing the entire neoplasm in most cases. Second, surgical excision is easy to perform and with proper wound care and utilization of an Elizabethan collar, the operation is almost always successful. The last reason involves the client's desire to rid his pet of an unsightly mass. Recurrence of the mass, however, can be a problem--one of which you should apprise your client. There is a catch, however. Recurrence depends on the type of tumor and you will not know what type of tumor you are dealing with until after you submit the tissue for histopath. The best you can do is advise your client on the chances of recurrence about 2 weeks after surgery, when the histopathologist reports the results to you. In general, lipomas and xanthomas, which are the most common, rarely reoccur, while the less common squamous cell carcinomas and adenocarcinomas will recur.

So that you will have an idea of what you will be seeing, the most common skin tumors will be described briefly (Fig. 10.1 provides information concerning distribution on the body). If a bird notices anything unusual, he will pick at it. At some point in this self-mutilation process, the bird will cry out with pain, and often this will be the first time the owner becomes aware of the problem, which now presents itself as a hemorrhaging mass. Many watchful owners, however, will observe the tumor earlier on, especially if the bird picks off the feathers around it before working on the tumor itself. If the mass gets large enough it will affect flight, walking, climbing, and balance. Most parakeets with tumor involvement, no matter where in the body, will not be afflicted until 2 years of age. Parrots show a 30-50 year range for tumor involvement.

Lipomas, the most common of all skin tumors, occur chiefly on the sternum, wings, and abdomen. They are yellow, turgid, and usually well encapsulated, often with a fluid center of friable, crumbly necrotic material. Budgies are very commonly afflicted with lipomas.

Xanthomas are also common, appearing as yellow discrete masses or diffuse, ulcerated thickenings of the skin. They are basically a mononuclear, inflammatory infiltration in response to accumulations of lipid droplets. Their cause is unknown. Distribution is mainly on the upper back, dorsal wing, and in the uropygial area.

Adenomas and adenocarcinomas of the preen gland occur frequently and probably are caused by nervous or "hyper" birds preening themselves excessively. Bleeding is often observed in the uropygial area. Since this region is highly vascular, surgical excision is usually augmented with a gelfoam pack to retard bleeding post-operatively.

Papillomas occur mainly on the neck, toes, mandible, and in the uropygial region. They are usually covered by a layer of dry, brown, crusty material which, if removed, reveals an elevated fleshy, vascular lesion.

Fibrosarcomas, found mostly on extremities near joints, are very common and can appear as early as one year of age in parakeets.

Finally, a number of non-neoplastic swellings may be confused with tumors. Near the joints of the feet and hock, shiny, creamy-yellow subcutaneous nodules causing swelling and severe pain are really the urate deposits of gout. Also, nodules on the bottom of the feet, resembling corns but containing pus, are the lesions of bumble-foot or staphylococcal infection.

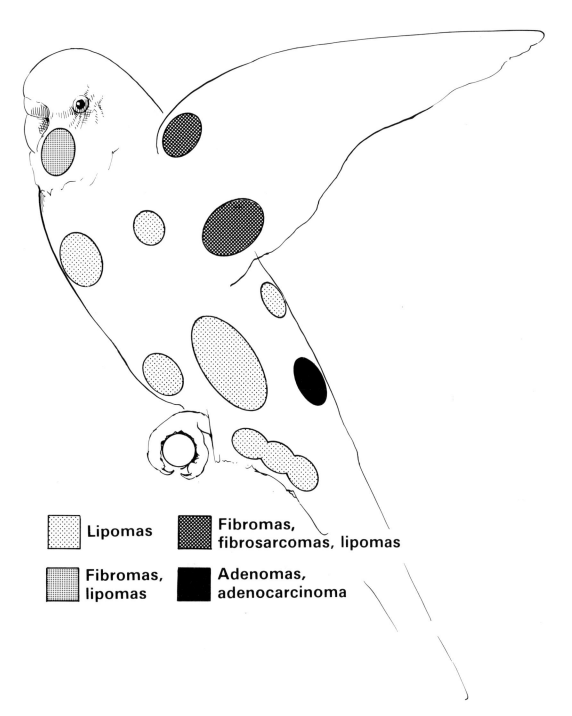

FIG. 10.1. Distribution of skin and subcutaneous neoplasms

ABDOMINAL TUMORS

Any time you find a bird with an abdominal lift, you should immediately suspect a space-occupying mass within the abdominal cavity. The mass will most likely be a tumor, but a bound egg, ascites, an ovarian cyst, or urate deposits of visceral gout could also be present. The abdominal lift is commonly caused by repositioning of the gizzard by the tumor mass so that the gizzard, normally located to the left and slightly caudal to the sternum, is pushed up directly under the sternum, lifting it away from the backbone and pubic bones. In some cases the tumor itself may push against the sternum, creating a lift. The normal distance between the caudal point of the sternum, called the xiphisternum, and the free ends of the pubic bones of a parakeet is 5 millimeters or about ¼ inch. Slight increases over this distance must be evaluated carefully, while substantial measurements over 5 millimeters indicate a definite lift, suggesting a space-occupying mass (Fig. 10.2). Just what exactly is causing the lift will require careful palpation, radiography, abdominocentesis, or even a laporatomy. A fluctuant, fluid-filled abdomen may indicate ascites of right-heart failure or hypoproteinemia, while signs of tenesmus and exhaustion may suggest a bound egg. Changes are good, however, that a neoplasm will be the cause of the lift.

Long before the abdomen shows enlargement, diffuse or malignant tumors of the liver and kidney generally produce a wasting disease. The signs seen are those associated with indigestion, such as diarrhea and watery, yellowish-white droppings. In taking a history then, be sure to ask if such signs were noticed prior to an abdominal lift occurring. Also, gradual onset will be the hallmark of most abdominal neoplasms.

Other signs of abdominal neoplasia besides an abdominal lift include panting, gasping, tiring quickly, fainting attacks (syncope), nervous fits, anorexia, constipation, diarrhea, weight loss, and exhaustion. Pressure on the sciatic nerves often gives rise to a leg paralysis. One very curious sign seen in birds with significant abdominal distention occurs when they perch. To keep from falling over backwards due to a more caudal center of gravity, the bird will perch in a horizontal position on its breast--a very unusual sight. Waddling is also seen when the bird attempts to walk.

Abdominal neoplasms of parakeets can be seen as early as 2 years of age. Unlike treatment of skin tumors, treatment of abdominal tumors is generally unproductive. By the time the abdominal lift is large enough to suggest the presence of a mass, the tumor has metastasized and involves most of the visceral organs. In such a condition, most birds will not tolerate the extensive surgery required. Euthanasia is strongly recommended.

Most abdominal tumors are adenocarcinomas of the kidney, embryonal nephromas, or gonadal tumors. Fibrosarcomas of the liver and lipomas occur less frequently.

BONE TUMORS

Fibromas, fibrosarcomas, and osteosarcomas are very commonly seen in caged birds, occurring mainly on the legs, wings, and occasionally

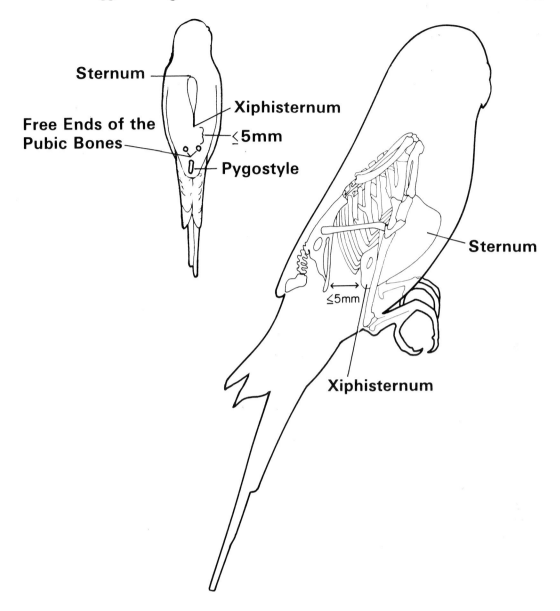

Sternum

Xiphisternum

≤5mm

**Free Ends of the
Pubic Bones**

Pygostyle

Sternum

≤5mm

Xiphisternum

FIG. 10.2. The five millimeter rule for the determination
of abdominal enlargement in a parakeet.

the ribs (Fig. 10.3). When malignancy is suspected, the only hope of
saving the bird's life is amputation of the limb well above the
growth. This may present a serious problem if a leg is involved. In
general, any tumor in or near a joint can be considered malignant.

As far as we know from our literature search, no one has had any
success with radiation or chemotherapy as a means of controlling neoplasia in the bird.

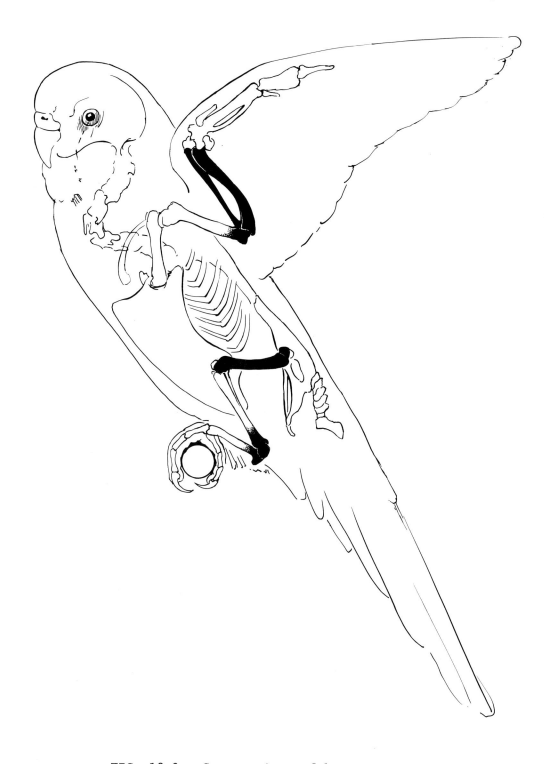

FIG. 10.3. Common sites of bone tumors.

EGG-BINDING

    Since abdominal distention is a central issue in the previous
section on neoplasia, egg-binding will also be discussed. The signs
of egg-binding, besides abdominal distention, include straining,
exhaustion, sudden onset of depression, and often cloacal or oviduct
prolapse. A history of recent egg laying is frequently reported. In
advanced cases the bird may stop passing feces or become septic due
to infection surrounding the bound egg. Hopefully, you will be able
to palpate the bound egg. A radiograph would prove highly diagnostic.

    The causes of egg-binding are numerous. Most causes ultimately
lead to spasm or atony of the oviduct (remember: only the left ovary
and oviduct develop in birds) which impedes the progress of an egg to
the outside. The chief causes of egg-binding are as follows:

    1. Chilling caused by drafty, damp nesting quarters or poor
nutrition may affect the normal functioning of the oviduct. Spasms or
cramps of the oviduct result. If the normal progress of the ovum down
the oviduct is interrupted or reversed due to spasms of the oviduct,
excessive amounts of albumin can be deposited or sometimes a double
shell may be laid down. Such an abnormally large egg may be passed
with difficulty or not at all.

    2. Calcium deficiency, along with chilling, is thought to be a
major cause of egg-binding. This conclusion has been drawn mainly
from the response to calcium therapy in egg-bound birds. Apparently,
contraction of smooth muscle in the uterus is enhanced by calcium,
increasing uterine tone. Also, several clinicians have noticed a
correlation between the lack of a cuttlebone and egg-binding in hens,
supporting calcium deficiency as a possible etiology.

    3. Salpingitis, or inflammation of the oviduct, usually due to
a bacterial infection with E. coli, increases production of mucus as
well as causing spasms in the oviduct which, as mentioned, causes
excessive albumin and egg shell deposition.

    4. Single or isolated pet hens often are offered no suitable
place to lay and therefore refuse to lay developing eggs.

    5. Older hens frequently become egg-bound, not because of ovi-
duct spasms, but because of atony of the oviduct.

    6. Exhaustion from over-breeding or out-of-season breeding
causes both spasms and atony of the oviduct.

    7. Obesity plays a very important role in egg-binding. In
general, fat birds lack vigor and good health, and often exhibit
irregular egg cycling and a spastic oviduct.

    So what can you do for an egg-bound bird? Before attempting
manual extrusion or surgery, give calcium borogluconate in saline,
subcutaneously. An effective dose has not been established, although
quite a variety of doses have been tried with considerable success.
Sedation or anesthesia may relax the oviduct and abdominal muscles to
the extent that you can manually extrude the bound egg by massage.
This can probably be done on an unsedated bird if the owner is absent.
Lubrication of the cloaca and oviduct with mineral oil may help in a
small number of cases, but is not enthusiastically recommended because
the feathers frequently become matted, losing their insulation effect

and leaving the bird prone to chilling. If manual manipulation is not
productive, a celiotomy and hysterotomy can be performed and the egg
removed.

QUESTIONS

Tumors
   1.   Which vertebrate animal has the highest incidence of neo-
        plasia?
   2.   Which order of the class Aves has the highest incidence of
        neoplasia? The lowest incidence?
   3.   What are the three categories of tumors in caged birds?
   4.   What is the ratio of malignant to benign neoplasms in caged
        birds?
   5.   What is the most common skin tumor? Where does this tumor
        occur most frequently?
   6.   What is the treatment for skin tumors? What is the progno-
        sis?
   7.   What special precaution must be taken when removing a tumor
        in the uropygial area?
   8.   What non-neoplastic conditions of the skin can be confused
        with tumors?
   9.   What are the signs associated with an abdominal tumor?
  10.   Name five conditions in pet birds which cause abdominal
        distention.
  11.   What is an abdominal lift? Describe the landmarks used in
        measuring this lift. Give the normal limits.
  12.   What two organs in the abdominal cavity are most often affec-
        ted by neoplasms?
  13.   What are the early signs associated with liver and kidney
        neoplasms?
  14.   What is the prognosis for abdominal neoplasia?
  15.   What treatment is recommended for tumors of the abdomen?
  16.   Where do bone tumors most commonly occur?
  17.   What is the treatment for a bone tumor?

Egg-Binding
   1.   What are the signs of egg-binding?
   2.   What diagnostic aid is helpful in establishing a diagnosis of
        egg-binding?
   3.   What is the ultimate cause of egg-binding in birds?
   4.   Name seven factors which predispose a bird to egg-binding.
   5.   What is the therapy for egg-bound birds?

CHAPTER 11

PSITTACOSIS

Psittacosis, the chlamydial disease of psittacine birds, is a true zoonotic disease: it is directly transmissible from the infected bird to man. To protect yourself and your clients it is critical that you understand this disease well.

The etiologic agent of psittacosis is a rickettsial organism, _Chlamydia psittaci_. It is an obligate, intracellular parasite, reproducing by binary fission with characteristic clusters of elementary bodies developing in infected cells. Its size is between that of a bacterium and virus, so that routine culture techniques used by a practioner might miss the organism. As with most Rickettsiae, _Chlamydia_ are susceptible to antibiotics, particularly tetracyclines, which arrest their multiplication.

The terminology applied to this condition is confusing, so we offer you the following straightforward, clear explanation. If the patient is a psittacine bird, the chlamydial disease is called psittacosis. If the patient is any other avian, the term ornithosis (literally "bird disease") applies. When man has contracted the disease, the condition is called psittacosis, regardless of which reservoir host was the source. The term psittacosis is preferred for the human condition, because traditionally human illness seemed to follow contact with psittacine birds. For the same reason, the now-abandoned term "Parrot Fever" was once used. Whatever disease we are speaking of, they are _all_ caused by the same agent, _Chlamydia psittaci_. You will also see the generic names _Miyagawanella_ and _Bedsonia_ used, but they are incorrect.

It has been observed that numerous strains of _Chlamydia psittaci_ exist, each with a different virulence. Apparently, each strain generates a toxin which has much to do with the virulence of the strain. Coupled with this variable virulence is the fact that species susceptibility within the avian group is also variable. Of the common cage birds, parrots, parakeets, and pigeons are considered relatively resistant but are natural reservoirs. Other non-psittacine cage birds are highly susceptible and are quick to contract ornithosis from a psittacine reservoir.

113

TRANSMISSION

Transmission occurs chiefly by means of inspiration of infected airborne droplets associated with nasal discharges. Contaminated droppings and feather dust can spread the organism via the oral route.

SIGNS

Generally, psittacosis, a systemic disease characterized by a septicemia, presents few or no signs in older birds. It is the younger birds that are the most susceptible and apt to develop full-fledged signs and a fatal infection. They are also the principal spreaders of the disease. The signs of psittacosis are described below:

1. Early, nonspecific signs.
   a. Depression
   b. Ruffled feathers
   c. Anorexia
   d. Rapid weight loss
   e. Watery diarrhea - organism is commonly shed in feces at this time
2. One to two weeks.
   a. ↓ quantity of feces
   b. Feces become a dark, yellow-green color and tenacious, soiling the plumage
3. Three weeks.
   a. Abundant feces - white and watery
   b. Mucopurulent nasal discharge
   c. Sneezing and headshaking
   d. Eyes may be pasted shut from dried exudate
   e. Rarely, tremors and paralysis of legs and wings
   f. Severe dehydration and emaciation → death

All or just a few of the above signs may be seen. The mortality is 10-100%, depending on the species of bird and the virulence of the strain of the chlamydial organism.

Birds that recover almost always continue to eliminate the organism in their discharges, continuously or intermittently, for long periods of time. It is these birds that perpetuate the disease by infecting the younger birds of the flock. Recovered birds are very healthy or may occasionally suffer from transient diarrhea. The carrier state is commonly discovered after the pet owner himself develops psittacosis.

GROSS LESIONS

A postmortem exam will usually provide much information. ALWAYS WEAR GLOVES AND A MASK FOR YOUR OWN PROTECTION. The gross lesions, which often form a characteristic pattern, are as follows:

1. Greatly enlarged spleen which may be soft and gray.
2. Swollen, friable liver with rounded edges and focal necrosis.
3. Airsacculitis.
4. Exudative pericarditis.
5. Congestion of the intestinal tract, particularly the serosa.

DIAGNOSIS

You, as a practitioner, can arrive at a tentative diagnosis based on signs and gross lesions. To confirm the diagnosis you will need the help of a sophisticated laboratory. If blood is available, a complement-fixation test can be run. Most of the time, however, an adequate volume of blood is not available, especially if the bird is a finch or a parakeet.

You should isolate the infected tissues and place half of them in 10% formalin for subsequent histopathologic study. The histopathologist will section the spleen, liver, and air sacs and stain them with Macchiavello's preparation. A positive stain shows red coccoid organisms within the cytoplasm of infected cells. The other half of infected tissues should be placed in a sterile whirl bag, refrigerated or frozen, and sent to the proper lab for culture and identification.

If you wish, you can make your own diagnostic impression smear from air sacs or the pericardium, or any exudate on these tissues. The smears are stained by the Macchiavello's method:
1. Air dry and fix the smear by very gentle heat.
2. Stain 5 to 10 minutes in 0.25% basic fuchsin.
3. Decolorize for 2-3 seconds in 0.25% citric acid.
4. Counterstain 30 seconds in 1% methylene blue.
5. View under oil, looking for intracytoplasmic red colonies in blue host cells.

A variety of culture techniques are used, but animal inoculation seems favored. Mice are inoculated intraperitoneally and when they die, imprints are made of their livers, a Macchiavello's stain is applied, and the organism sought. Above all, never attempt to culture Chlamydia psittaci yourself. You will only be asking for trouble.

TREATMENT AND PROPHYLAXIS

If you have definitively diagnosed psittacosis in a flock (based on clinical signs and postmortem tests done on infected tissues) a special dilemma faces you. If the flock cannot be isolated from humans, a prudent decision would be to destroy all infected birds. The rationale for such a move is that even with prolonged treatment the chlamydial organisms will persist, creating a carrier bird which could transmit the disease to a human. On the other hand, persistent treatment of a valuable bird which can be isolated may be warranted, if periodic prophylactic treatment is continued the rest of the bird's life. The decision will be up to the owner. Just remember to fully apprise him of the zoonotic significance of psittacosis.

Treatment with tetracyclines arrests the multiplication of Chlamydia psittaci and can totally suppress it, but never eliminate it. Prolonged therapy, as long as 45 days in length, is required since tetracyclines inhibit rather than inactivate the organism. Chlortetracycline (CTC) has proven highly efficacious and is readily absorbed in the GI tract. Its use in the feed, therefore, is ideal since minimum manipulation of infected birds is required. Chlortetracycline-impregnated millet [0.5 mg CTC per gram of millet (Keet-Life[R])] is commercially available for treatment of parakeets. If the

bird is so sick that it will not eat, 5-10 mg of injectable tetracycline may be given intramuscularly SID the first few days. Such a
sick bird, however, poses a great threat to the handler. When the
bird feels better, CTC-impregnated millet should be continued for at
least 15 or 30 days, or longer if signs remain moderate to severe.
If other birds are present they should be treated prophylactically
along with the sick bird.

The above therapeutic regimen applies to parakeets and other
small, seed-eating birds, such as canaries and finches. Psittacines
larger than parakeets will not subsist on a diet of millet only, so
a different diet is needed, and to obtain satisfactory blood levels
the concentration of CTC in the feed must be increased to 4-10 mg/gm
(0.4 to 1%).

There are two components to this parrot treatment. One is a feed
base in which you mix the CTC. It consists of rice and hen scratch
(hen scratch can be purchased at any feed store). The second compo-
nent is a common commercial formulation of 22% chlortetracycline mixed
in soybean meal, known as Aureomycin SF 66^R (Lederle). This 22% CTC/
soybean meal mixture works out to be 100 gm of CTC per pound of soybean meal. Using the feed base of rice and hen scratch with 22% CTC
in soybean meal, you can direct your client to prepare a diet as outlined by Bankowski et al. (1977). They suggest cooking two parts hen
scratch, two parts rice, and three parts water in a pressure cooker
for 10-15 minutes, until soft (for example, 1 pound scratch and 1
pound rice in 1½ pints of water). After cooling, add the Aureomycin
SF 66 in an amount equal to 2% of the weight of the cooked feed mixture. Stir in some brown sugar to increase palatability. The result-
ant ration will contain 4.4 mg CTC/gm of cooked feed. Give the bird
as much as it will eat in one day, with the objective of ultimately
giving one-fifth of its body weight each day, but this will be variable. Within a few days adequate blood levels of CTC will be reached.

No other feeds should be given during the treatment periods and
insure fresh water is always available. A separate dish containing a
mixture of a coarse sand or gravel with a vitamin and mineral supplement (non-medicated broiler starter-grower crumbles) should also be
provided.

The CTC medicated ration must be prepared daily and administered
exclusively for 30 days, or preferably 45 days. Such a regimen is
also recommended as a periodic prophylactic treatment for well birds
and new additions.

A ready-made, CTC-nutrient pellet is used by federal monitors
at ports of entry to control psittacosis, but as yet it is not available commercially.

Of course, if a parrot or other large psittacine is too sick to
eat, a dosage level of any parenteral tetracycline of 40-50 mg IM can
be given daily until the bird begins to eat. Again, the handler is
at great risk and should wear a mask and gloves.

Nectar-feeding birds, such as lories and lorikeets, must be given
a liquid preparation. To the ration described in Chapter 4, Nutrition
of Caged Birds, add the contents of a tetracycline or chlortetracycline capsule so that one liter of ration contains 500 mg of antibiotic. Offer only this medicated ration for 30-45 days.

OTHER BENEFITS OF CHEMOTHERAPY

Of the approximately 3 million pet birds sold at the retail level each year, 70% are prophylactically treated with CTC. Not only has a significant decline in psittacosis occurred, but the vigor and plumage have been seen to improve following completion of the chemotherapy. The probable explanation is that subclinical bacterial or mycoplasmal infections are being controlled by CTC.

A critical discovery by Tribby (1973) indicates that no amount of therapy will ever completely rid the bird of chlamydial organisms. Apparently, the inhibitory effect of CTC on chlamydial multiplication is reversible. Even though biochemical pathways within the organism are brought to a standstill the organism persists in a dormant form and is able to slowly regenerate those pathways when therapy is discontinued. So periodic 30-45 day prophylactic treatments with CTC are warranted throughout the bird's life to keep the infection in check.

IMPORT REGULATIONS

In 1971 to protect the poultry industry from exotic Newcastle disease, psittacosis, and other communicable diseases, the Animal and Plant Health Inspection Service of the United States Department of Agriculture was assigned the task of regulating importation of all birds into the United States.

The requirements for the importation of commercial birds into the U.S. are as follows:
1. An import permit must be obtained in advance of shipment.
2. A health certificate must be issued by a full-time, salaried veterinarian in the government of the country from which the birds are shipped.
3. Each lot must be quarantined for a minimum period of 30 days in a facility provided by the importer in the immediate facility of the port of entry.
4. During the quarantine period, all exotic birds of the psittacine family must receive treatment with CTC as a precautionary measure against psittacosis.

QUESTIONS
1. What is the difference between psittacosis and ornithosis?
2. What is the cause of psittacosis? Ornithosis?
3. How is psittacosis transmitted?
4. What are the signs of psittacosis?
5. What are the gross lesions of psittacosis?
6. Can you obtain a positive diagnosis in your clinic? If so, how?
7. How is a positive diagnosis obtained in a lab?
8. Why is euthanasia the preferred method of dealing with birds infected with psittacosis?

9. Briefly describe the treatment (drug, dose, duration) for psittacosis in:
    a. Parakeets and small, seed-eating birds
    b. Large psittacines
    c. Nectar-eating birds
10. How does chlortetracycline work to control Chlamydia psittaci? What is the significance regarding elimination of the organism according to Tribby?

CHAPTER 12

PACHECO'S DISEASE

A client calls to ask what could possibly have caused his love-bird to die. The lovebird, which he purchased a couple of weeks ago from a local, high-volume pet store, was in excellent health last evening and found dead this morning. A brief discussion concerning lovebird husbandry and management convinces you the client provided a safe and adequate environment for his pet bird. You are permitted to necropsy the bird and find no visible lesions. What then killed this lovebird?

Several weeks later a lady owning a private aviary reports she has lost nine birds (4 cockatiels, 2 parakeets, 2 macaws, and 1 cocka-too) over the past 3 weeks and is desperate. You visit the aviary where you learn that each bird died suddenly within 1-2 days after showing signs of diarrhea and 4-8 hours after becoming depressed. Necropsy of the bird which died that morning reveals a very subtle mottling of the liver. With further investigation, you are told of the most recent addition, a young Military Macaw, which arrived 5 weeks ago from a distributor in Atlanta. One observation you make on your own is that none of the finches, Mynah birds, or Golden Seabright Bantam chickens present in the collection have been affected by the disease.

Presented with these two very typical cases in which psittacine birds die suddenly of a generalized, non-descript malaise, often with no gross lesions, most of today's practitioners would be lost. But you won't be, because, among your rule-outs, you have included Pacheco's disease or inclusion body hepatitis of psittacines.

HISTORY

In November of 1929 a bird park in São Paulo, Brazil was suffer-ing great losses in its parrot population. Psittacosis, a highly fatal parrot disease, the pathogenesis of which was incompletely known at that time, was believed to be the disease involved. Dr. Genesio Pacheco of the Biological Institute of São Paulo was called in to confirm psittacosis as the cause. The signs Dr. Pacheco noted were lethargy, droopy eyes, ruffled feathers, and a reluctance to

move, followed by death. His postmortem exam was negative, but he did
find, on histopathologic exam, areas of focal necrosis in the livers
and kidneys with eosinophilic, intranuclear inclusion bodies in hepatic and renal tubular cells.

Confused, Dr. Pacheco sent infected liver tissue to Drs. Rivers
and Schwenker at the Rockefeller Institute for Medical Research in
New York for characterization of the agent. In 1931 they concluded
that the agent was a virus, specific to parrots and parakeets, and was
unrelated to the agent causing psittacosis either in birds or man.
The disease became known as Pacheco's parrot disease.

That was the last Pacheco's virus or Pacheco's disease was heard
from for 45 years. During the next half century, the importation of
exotic birds into the United States became a big business, with more
and more attention given to their disease problems. Basically, the
exotic bird importers did not wish to diminish their profits from
dying birds, while the U. S. poultry industry became concerned over a
possible epidemic of Newcastle disease which might be brought into the
country by exotic birds.

In 1974, four young macaws were introduced into a flock of 10
resident macaws at Disney World. Three of the new macaws died within
7 days and 4 of the resident macaws and 12 cockatoos in an adjacent
flight died within 12-14 days. Simpson and Hanley, researchers from
the University of Florida, were consulted. They found that the only
evidence of sickness was lethargy shortly before death. They found no
significant gross lesions. Successful in producing the disease by
injection of infected tissue from dead birds into isolated, "clean"
parakeets and using other tests, they determined the agent to be a
Herpesvirus, causing hepatic necrosis and eosinophilic intranuclear
inclusions in hepatocytes. At last, the exact etiologic agent of
Pacheco's disease was known.

Since that time, outbreaks of Pacheco's disease have been reported in Kenya, Thailand, Europe, Los Angeles, Chicago, Houston and
Atlanta, suggesting a worldwide distribution.

SIGNS AND GROSS LESIONS
The signs of Pacheco's disease usually follow a definite pattern.
Yellowish, watery diarrhea occurs 1-2 days before death and depression
only hours before death. When death occurs, it happens amazingly
fast. Frequently there is no diarrhea, with death occurring acutely
2-4 hours after the warning sign of depression appears. If the owner
misses the depression phase, all he will see is a dead bird. Acute
death is the hallmark of Pacheco's disease.

In the depression phase, inactivity, anorexia, lethargy, frequent
prolonged closing of the eyes, ruffled feathers, and a preference for
the cage floor rather than a perch are commonly seen. Since watery
diarrhea, followed by these nonspecific signs of depression and acute
death, are generalized signs consistent with many systemic conditions
(such as psittacosis or abdominal neoplasia) you cannot tell the
client anything specific without a thorough, meticulous necropsy, although you should suspect Pacheco's disease.

At necropsy you will often find no significant lesions with Pacheco's disease, especially if you don't know what to look for. On the other hand, psittacosis, the other major rule-out to be considered, may show a nasal discharge and some diarrhea, with a greatly enlarged spleen, an airsacculitis, an exudative pericarditis, and occasionally a swollen, discolored, friable liver. Commonly, however, Pacheco's cases will also have livers that are slightly discolored, but with tiny focal areas of necrosis and petechial hemorrhages. Some birds exhibit only a very subtle, diffuse mottling of the liver, the lesions being centrilobular necrosis. On gross lesions alone you can consider Pacheco's disease, but you must also rule out a hepatitis of toxic, bacterial, or viral (other than Pacheco's virus) origin.

(WHENEVER EXAMINING A SICK BIRD, ESPECIALLY AN IMPORTED COMPANION BIRD, YOU SHOULD ALWAYS HAVE NEWCASTLE DISEASE AS ONE OF YOUR RULE-OUTS. VISCEROTROPIC, VELOGENIC NEWCASTLE DISEASE CAUSES DIARRHEA, SWELLING OF THE HEAD AND NECK, AND OFTEN CNS SIGNS WITH GROSS LESIONS OF HEMORRHAGE IN THE GI TRACT.)

DIAGNOSIS

A suddenly lethargic psittacine has died and you are fortunate enough to find a necrotic hepatitis on necropsy. At this point you can make only a presumptive diagnosis of Pacheco's disease. For confirmation, a histopathologic exam is required. With Pacheco's disease a diffuse necrosis of hepatic parenchyma and hemorrhage will be present, even if no gross lesions are evident. The pathognomonic finding is the presence of intranuclear inclusion bodies in hepatocytes. The intranuclear inclusion can be either a solid, basophilic body filling the entire nucleus or an eosinophilic, centrally-located body separated from the marginated chromatin by a clear halo. By EM studies, these intranuclear inclusions are known to be aggregates of viral particles. The lesion diagnosis you would receive from a trained avian histopathologist would read, "There is a diffuse, necrotizing inclusion body hepatitis with hemorrhage, indicative of Pacheco's disease." If the pathognomonic inclusion body is not present the report will read, "There is a diffuse, necrotizing hepatitis with hemorrhage, suggestive of Pacheco's Disease."

Occasionally, intranuclear inclusions are found in renal tubular epithelium and in gut epithelium, but their significance is not known. Importantly, a finding of one intranuclear inclusion in one affected hepatocyte is all that is required for a positive diagnosis. Virus isolation is the ultimate method to confirm the presence of Pacheco's virus. This should be done on frozen hepatic, renal, intestinal, and fecal samples you have sent to a state lab.

TRANSMISSION AND INFECTION SOURCE

The herpesvirus of Pacheco's disease is shed in the feces and transmitted most often orally, through contaminated food, in contaminated water, or by preening contaminated plumage. If two groups of birds are in adjacent cages, one group infected and one healthy, the disease cannot be transmitted unless there is fecal contamination. If uncleaned food and water containers are switched from one cage to the other, the disease can be transmitted. This is one way pet shops and wholesalers may transmit the disease.

There are two basic sources of Pacheco's virus. One is a shedding, sick bird before it dies (and it will die if it shows signs). The other source is assymptomatic carriers which are totally resistant to the disease but harbor the virus. Certain types of conures, particularly the Pattigonian conures, are believed to be such carriers.

The incubation period for Pacheco's disease is variable. The large psittacines can show signs within 4½ days after exposure. On the other extreme, the incubation period may extend into years for other psittacines, with signs appearing when severe stress occurs.

TREATMENT

There is no treatment for Pacheco's disease. Birds which have Pacheco's virus and show signs always die. Realistically, you will probably not even see a bird sick with Pacheco's disease unless you have schooled your clients well in the need for early treatment of any pet bird illness. In most cases you will be trying to find out why a bird has died, utilizing a postmortem exam and subsequent histopathology. You may feel there is little demand for such a service, but quite to the contrary, most pet bird owners have an intense desire to know why their bird succumbed and often insist on a careful necropsy.

PREVENTION

Prevention, as in the case with most avian diseases, provides the best hope of sparing psittacine birds the ravages of Pacheco's disease. Stricter and longer quarantine periods at the port of entry will eliminate many infected birds. Asymptomatic carriers, however, will remain a problem. Standard for the prevention of any avian disease should be a self-imposed quarantine period by anyone owning more than one bird. All new birds being introduced should be isolated and observed for a minimum of 6 weeks. Again, carriers will circumvent this protective measure.

With the knowledge that transmission occurs orally by ingestion of contaminated feces and that psittacines love to climb, specific prevention measures are obvious. Where possible, use a wire bottom cage so contaminated droppings fall out of the cage. Cover food and water containers with a hood. Keep all perches at the same height so one bird can't soil another bird. Reduce a bird's ability to climb and do not overcrowd.

An ideal prevention would be a vaccine but none is available at this time.

CONCLUSIONS

Pacheco's disease is poorly understood mainly because so little research has been conducted. Based on observations made during

recent outbreaks, the following conclusions can be drawn:
1. The disease has worldwide distribution.
2. Only psittacine birds are susceptible.
3. Susceptible birds are often young.
4. Affected birds usually have been stressed in some way.
5. The existence of assymptomatic carriers seems quite likely.
6. Humans are not affected by Pacheco's virus.
7. Poultry are not affected by Pacheco's virus.

As a matter of interest, there is a disease called Inclusion Body Hepatitis of Chickens, caused by an adenovirus not the Herpesvirus of Pacheco's disease. There is also an Inclusion Body Hepatitis of Owls and an Inclusion Body Hepatitis of Falcons. Each of these diseases is species specific.

QUESTIONS
1. What is the cause of Pacheco's disease?
2. What type of bird does Pacheco's disease affect? Give examples.
3. What are the signs of Pacheco's disease?
4. What are the major rule-outs, when considering only the signs?
5. What are the gross lesions of Pacheco's disease?
6. What lesions will you find on histopath?
7. Which microscopic lesion is pathognomonic?
8. How do you treat Pacheco's disease?
9. What prevents quarantine from halting the spread of Pacheco's disease?
10. How is Pacheco's disease transmitted?
11. How can the spread of Pacheco's disease be prevented?

CHAPTER 13

NEWCASTLE DISEASE

A very serious and highly infectious avian disease, Newcastle disease, was first described by Doyle in 1927 as a fatal viral disease of domestic poultry occurring near Newcastle-upon-Tyne, England. The etiological agent was determined to be a paramyxo virus which survives for long periods under favorable temperature and humidity conditions. Newcastle disease is also called Fowl or Avian Pest, Avian Distemper, and Ranikhet Disease. Its distribution is worldwide.

Newcastle disease is primarily considered to be a disease of gallinaceous birds but it does have a large range of other susceptible avian hosts, including pheasants, partridges, quail, owls, pigeons, and psittacines. Several epidemics in Africa have devastated parrot populations in localized areas. Newcastle disease also occurs naturally in finches, sparrows, starlings and canaries.

Numerous strains of the Newcastle disease virus (NDV) exist, each with a different virulence and each having a variable disease impact on the different avian species. It is generally accepted that caged birds come down with Newcastle disease by one of two ways:

1. The caged bird becomes infected by contact with infected poultry, especially chickens. This usually occurs in the country of origin prior to export to the United States. The test and slaughter method of Newcastle disease control is generally not practiced or not strictly enforced in the country of origin. If a slightly virulent strain of NDV infects an exotic bird in this manner, there is a chance that manifestation of the disease may not occur until after the mandatory quarantine period in the United States, owing to a variable incubation period.

2. Caged birds may contract an avirulent or a nearly avirulent strain of NDV which, ordinarily, would not cause any disease (making the bird an assymptomatic carrier). But with the stress of shipping and quarantine, what little resistance to Newcastle disease the bird possesses will disappear and signs of disease will become evident. The effect is to upgrade the virus from an avirulent type to one of slight or medium virulence.

Despite the evidence supporting a wide species susceptibility, it is generally accepted that caged birds have some innate resistance

125

to Newcastle disease. But then all it takes to bring economic
disaster to the U. S. poultry industry is one nonresistant psittacine,
so the quarantine vigil is strictly enforced. Unfortunately, little
can be done to stop the spread of NDV from Mexico and the Carribean
Islands by wild birds. A vigorous vaccination program by the poultry
industry has been the answer so far.

NEWCASTLE DISEASE VIRUS (NDV)
     Newcastle disease is not one but a series of clinical entities,
ranging from a fulminating fatal illness to an inapparent carrier
state. The form of the disease is determined primarily by the strain
of the virus. All Newcastle disease viruses are placed in one of five
categories based on virulence and signs:
     1. Velogenic viscerotropic Newcastle disease (VVND) - also call-
ed Asiatic Newcastle disease. VVND produces rapid and high mortality
and principally affects the GI tract, producing hemorrhage and a
greenish, mucoid diarrhea, with swelling and edema of the head.
     2. Velogenic neurotropic Newcastle disease - formerly called
pneumoencephalitis and now sometimes referred to as American Newcastle
disease. Neurotropic Newcastle disease initially affects the lower
respiratory tree causing pneumonia, bronchitis, and tracheitis: within a few days it causes a non-suppurative encephalitis which deva-
states the bird. Incoordination, tremors, paresis, torticollis,
prostration, and, finally, death are the signs. Morbidity and mortality are both high.
     3. Mesogenic Newcastle disease - caused by less pathogenic
strains of NDV. GI signs are not seen. Nervous signs are evident,
but are not as severe as in neurotropic Newcastle disease. Mortality
is low.
     4. Lentogenic Newcastle disease - although the bird is infected,
signs are not common and mortality is extremely rare.
     5. Inapparent, carrier state of Newcastle disease - this strain
of NDV is avirulent to the species it has infected and produces no
signs and no mortality. The problem arises when the carrier bird
passes this strain of virus to another species of bird. Disease and
mortality are often the result.
     The above classification of NDV is based on the disease entities
seen in domestic poultry. Caged birds show a similar variation in
signs, due mainly to differential susceptibility among species of
caged birds and the multiplicity of strains of NDV.

SIGNS OF NEWCASTLE DISEASE IN CAGED BIRDS
     In caged birds look for four basic types of signs or a combina-
tion of these signs:
     1. Respiratory signs
     2. Depression and diarrhea
     3. Nervous signs
     4. Sudden death

Most often Newcastle disease in caged birds will be severe, resulting in sudden death. Commonly, however, the bird will appear very ill for a few days, showing respiratory involvement, anorexia, depression, ruffled feathers with profuse ocular and nasal discharge, and conjunctivitis. Gasping respiration is an early sign. Yellow to green diarrhea may be seen as a lone sign or it may be observed with respiratory signs.

Birds which survive the respiratory and GI insult may develop a viral encephalitis and show ataxia, wing tremors, torticollis, paralysis of extremities, nodding and jerking of the head, muscular twitching, or abnormal posture. Birds with these signs usually die, but may recover and continue to shed the virus for over a year. Frequently, the neurological form of Newcastle disease is manifested without any respiratory or visceral signs.

GROSS AND HISTOPATHOLOGIC LESIONS

Birds which die acutely often show no gross lesions. Other birds may show a catarrhal tracheitis with or without hemorrhage, a diffuse enteritis, congestion, hemorrhage, and necrosis of the GI tract, particularly the proventriculus, or a combination of these lesions. Serous to fibrinous peritonitis and ascites have also been reported.

Microscopically, the brain will show gliosis, satellitosis and perivascular cuffing with lymphocytes, all indicative of a non-suppurative encephalitis. There are no gross lesions in the central nervous system. The trachea and bronchi will show squamous metaplasia or hyperplasia of the respiratory epithelium, increased mucus production, and a submucosal, mononuclear inflammatory response.

DIAGNOSIS

Whenever there is mortality in aviary birds coupled with an outbreak of Newcastle disease in neighboring poultry flocks, your suspicions should be raised. NDV is shed in respiratory exudate and feces and is transmitted by direct contact with infected feed, drinking water, litter, or aerosolized secretions. It would be very easy for an assymptomatic wild bird to transport the virus from an infected poultry flock to an aviary.

To confirm Newcastle disease virus, isolation and identification must be performed. The demonstration of antibodies to NDV in the serum of live birds is also an important diagnostic aid. Affected tissues, lung and trachea (these two tissues usually have the highest virus titer), and brain (virus persists here long after it has disappeared from other sites), spleen, liver, kidney, and bone marrow should be frozen and sent to your state diagnostic lab for virus isolation. The lab will homogenize these tissues and inject them onto the chorioallantoic membrane of 9 to 11 day-old embryonating chicken eggs. Three days later the allantoic fluid containing the growing NDV can be harvested.

NDV, along with avian influenza virus and avian adenovirus, has hemagglutinating activity. The allantoic fluid, which hopefully contains the NDV, can be mixed with chicken red blood cells to see if agglutination occurs. This hemagglutination test (HA) is called the rapid plate test. One drop of allantoic fluid is mixed with 1 drop of a 5% suspension of washed red blood cells on a white porcelain plate. If clumping of the red blood cells occurs, one of three viruses is present: NDV, avian influenza virus, or avian adenovirus. The next step involves mixing immune serum (on hand in the lab) containing antibodies to Newcastle disease with the allantoic fluid. If this mixture fails to agglutinate chicken red blood cells, it can be said that the immune serum inhibited the virus in the allantoic fluid from agglutinating the red blood cells. With great specificity the Newcastle disease antibodies have tied up the NDV, rendering it incapable of hemagglutination. This is the hemagglutination-inhibition (HI) test. In a similar manner, using known Newcastle disease antigen, the HI test can be used to detect antibodies to Newcastle disease in the serum of live birds.

To recapitulate, diagnosis of Newcastle disease is accomplished by evaluation of clinical signs and gross lesions, by virus isolation and identification using infected tissues, and by detection of Newcastle disease antibodies in serum. In reality, this disease is uncommon in caged birds. But since it is so important to the poultry industry you must always be aware of its disease potential.

TREATMENT AND PREVENTION

There is no treatment for Newcastle disease. Control involves preventing a bird from ever coming into contact with the virus. This can be accomplished by isolation of healthy birds from infected birds. If such isolation is not possible, active immunity against NDV can be obtained by immunization with live or killed vaccines intended for poultry. We do not encourage the use of the live vaccine since the strain of NDV (mesogenic or lentogenic strain), used as a harmless antigen in poultry, may produce a fatal disease in caged birds. Whatever vaccine is used, immunity lasts only 90 days. Vaccination, therefore should be considered only in the face of a local outbreak of the disease.

Of course, the USDA's Animal Plant Health Inspection Service (APHIS) operates avian quarantine stations at all ports of entry to attempt to eliminate any caged bird which might have Newcastle disease. They are mainly looking for VVND or Asiatic Newcastle disease.

QUESTIONS
1. What other names does Newcastle disease go by?
2. What is the cause of Newcastle disease?
3. What is the significance of Newcastle disease in the U. S.?
4. What property of the etiologic agent aids in its identification?
5. What categories are the strains of NDV placed in? Briefly describe each.

6. What are the signs of Newcastle disease in caged birds?
7. How do caged birds usually contract Newcastle disease?
8. How is Newcastle disease transmitted?
9. What lesions, gross and microscopic, are seen?
10. What tissues should be submitted for VI?
11. What is the treatment for Newcastle disease?
12. What control measures are employed to prevent the disease?
13. If viral growth medium is HA positive, what viruses could be present? How would you confirm the presence of NDV?
14. Why are the signs and mortality of Newcatle disease so variable?

CHAPTER 14

ANESTHESIA OF CAGED BIRDS

The one factor which limits a practitioner from successfully examining and treating caged birds is his lack of training and experience with avian anesthesia. In this essay we will discuss those points about anesthesia which are critical to birds and we will provide several specific anesthetic regimes which have been tried and proven safe.

Without question, the anesthetic regime and technique can be more important to the success of an operation than the surgery itself. As a rule, anesthesia should be avoided if the surgical procedure can be accomplished without it. Several important points about avian anesthesia and surgery, therefore, should be kept in mind:

1. Because a bird has such a high metabolic rate, a fasting period will deplete the glycogen stores in the liver, decreasing hepatic detoxification capacity. As a result, the fasted birds do not tolerate anesthesia very well. Crop surgery will require fasting, however.

2. Birds should be kept warm (80-90°F) during the anesthetic experience and during recovery. Loss of body heat is rapid and often fatal.

3. For procedures longer than a half hour, fluid therapy is recommended. These long anesthetic episodes are prone to vascular collapse and circulatory failure and to dehydration, which occurs through the respiratory tract during inhalational anesthesia. Lactated Ringers solution can be given as a bolus intramuscularly every 10-15 minutes. An IV drip is ideal, but the fragility of veins, hematoma formation, and blood loss preclude its use. A parakeet can be given 0.1 ml of fluid IM every 10 minutes, selecting alternate sites with each administration.

4. As with mammals, monitoring the stage of anesthesia during surgery is critical. Since birds tend to become lost under large opaque drapes, the use of plastic transparent drapes permits easy visualization of the rate and depth of respiration. Heart rate should also be monitored with an esophageal stethoscope or an EKG oscilloscope.

5. The minimum data base prior to surgery should include a PCV and a blood glucose determination. If the PCV is $\geq$ 55 the bird should be rehydrated prior to surgery. A PCV of 20 or below indicates severe anemia. Surgery should either be postponed or a homologous blood transfusion given. If homologous blood is unavailable, pigeon blood may be used satisfactorily. (We have no experience with multiple transfusions, so incompatibility of blood types has not been addressed.) Blood glucose levels below 200 mg/100 ml require supplementation with 5% dextrose IV prior to surgery.

6. Administer atropine at a dosage of 0.04 to 0.1 mg/kg or 0.003 mg/30 gm bird to decrease the flow of respiratory secretions. A microliter syringe is an absolute necessity for this injection.

7. If at all possible, intubate every bird, no matter what size the bird is, no matter what the surgical procedure is, and no matter what type of anesthetic is used. If respiratory arrest occurs, you will be able to deal with it quickly and effectively.

8. Wing flapping, leg movement, or general excitatory behavior usually occur during recovery from anesthesia, so a quiet cage with a padded floor free of debris, waterers, or feeders should be provided. Birds should be kept warm and the body, legs, and wings wrapped loosely in a towel for protection. The head should be only partially included in the wrap. One or two low perches should be provided near each end. Recovery is quicker in full light.

9. Weak, debilitated birds, and older birds require less anesthetic to achieve the desired level of anesthesia. A good physical prior to anesthesia, therefore, is important in determining the dose of anesthetic to be used.

LOCAL ANESTHESIA

In general, local anesthetics are not widely used in birds, which have poor cutaneous sensation and a poor vascular system in their integument. They bleed very little and show little discomfort when the skin is incised. There are, however, several highly sensitive areas which may require local anesthesia. These sensitive areas - the head, cere, scaled parts of the legs, limb joints, and vent - are also useful in monitoring the depth of general anesthesia, since they are good sites to measure response to stimuli. Some local anesthetics recommended for use in birds are:

1. <u>Lidocaine hydrochloride aqueous</u> - <u>2%</u>. In large birds a volume of 1-3 ml may be used. A volume not exceeding 1 ml can be used in birds the size of pigeons. Use sparingly to avoid any systemic effect. It should not be used in small birds and epinephrine should never be added.

2. <u>Proparacaine hydrochloride</u> - <u>5%</u> (Ophthane[R] by Squibb). An ophthalmic topical anesthetic, it is very useful for detailed eye examinations.

3. <u>Lidocaine hydrochloride ointment</u> - <u>5%</u>. This is a good, basic, topical anesthetic which has proven very effective in reduction of prolapsed cloacas by reducing discomfort and providing lubrication.

4. Cetacaine[R] (from Cetylite Industries). This is a topical anesthetic mixture of ethyl aminobenzoate, butyl aminobenzoate, and tetracaine HCl. This topical anesthetic can be sprayed onto an abscess which needs lancing or on a prolapsed cloaca or oviduct. Cetacaine acts in one minute and lasts for 30 minutes. It paralyzes peripheral nerve endings and has some germicidal effect. Never use on or near the eye.

5. Ethylchloride. This is a topical anesthetic which evaporates so quickly that it freezes the area to which it is applied, functionally paralyzing peripheral nerve endings. It is very short-acting.

Procaine should not be used in caged birds. It will produce ataxia, seizures, and death. Very low doses are tolerated, but the margin of safety among species is so variable and generally so small that we do not recommend its use at all.

STAGES OF ANESTHESIA

1. Light anesthesia. Reflexes (palpebral, corneal, cere, pedal) are present; respiration is deep and rapid; there is no voluntary movement; there is no response to vibration or postural changes (proprioception has been abolished).

2. Medium anesthesia. Corneal and pedal reflexes are sluggish; palpebral and cere reflexes are absent; respiration is slow, deep, and regular; voluntary movement is absent. This stage of anesthesia is where most surgical procedures are performed.

3. Deep anesthesia. There is no voluntary movement and all reflexes are abolished; respiration is very slow, regular, but shallow. More anesthetic will cause respiratory arrest in this stage.

Assessment of what stage of anesthesia the bird is in is accomplished by evaluation of reflexes and respiration. The corneal and palpebral reflexes can be used but are not very reliable. Response to a stimulus, such as a pinch with forceps on the comb, wattles, cere, or interdigital web of the feet, is a very reliable indicator. The best gauge of anesthetic plane, however, is observation of the depth, rate, and pattern of respiration. In general, respiration in the medium stage of anesthesia, where most surgery is performed, will be slower than respiration in the awake bird, but just as smooth and rhythmic. Any sudden change in the rate, depth, or rhythm of respiration should signal an immediate evaluation of the anesthetic status of the bird. Usually a slower rate, but decreased depth, of respiration indicates the bird is getting too deep, while a faster rate with a increase in depth should suggest the bird is getting light. This is not always the case, however, so look to the reflexes for more information.

GENERAL ANESTHESIA--INHALATION

To produce general anesthesia, the inhalational method is preferred over the injectable method because control of the stage of anesthesia is easier. Injectable agents cannot be reversed and must be metabolized before their effect wears off.

Inhalational anesthetics can be administered by machine, by manual deposition of the agent (metafane) into the nares or mouth of the bird using a TB syringe (give to effect), or by placing the bird in a jar containing cotton which has been soaked with the agent. This last method is for small birds only; the skin and feathers should not be allowed to contact the anesthetic. Induction for larger birds can be accomplished by preanesthetizing them with ketamine or masking them down. If an anesthetic machine is to be used, an endotracheal tube with uninflated cuff, should be placed in position after induction, or a face mask may be used for maintenance. In all intubated birds connected to a machine, an Ayer's T-piece is recommended. It provides for an open, non-rebreathing system which is critical in birds because their tidal volume is so small they are unable to move anesthetic through a closed system. Endotracheal tubes for birds are not available commercially except for very large birds. You will have to resort to various types of soft tubing (catheters, etc.) available in your clinic. Of course, all endotracheal tubes should be moist or lubricated to facilitate safe intubation.

Occasionally you will encounter an ornery or combative bird that defies handling. Cover the cage with the bird in it with a large plastic trash bag and run the hose of your anesthetic machine into the bag. Turn on the gas and when the bird is induced, remove him from the cage and intubate him.

The three gas anesthesia regimes we recommend are outlined below:

1. Halothane--considered safest gas anesthetic because the stage of anesthesia can be adjusted and conrolled quickly; short induction period; rapid covery.

      Induction: Place bird's head into a mask
                     Halothane concentration: 2.5-3.0%
                     Oxygen flow: 0.5-2.0 liter/minute
                     Induction time: 3-4 minutes
   Maintenance: Halothane concentration: 0.5-1.5%
                     Oxygen flow: 0.5-1.0 liter/minute
                     Intubate larger birds to deliver anesthetic
                         directly into trachea
                     Small birds should remain masked
     Recovery: With 100% oxygen flow → 3-8 minutes

2. Halothane and nitrous oxide--smoother induction and more rapid recovery than halothane alone.

      Induction: Place bird's head into a mask
                     Halothane concentration: 3-4%
                     Oxygen flow: 1 liter/minute
                     Nitrous oxide flow: 1 liter/minute
   Maintenance: Intubate large birds/keep mask on small birds
                     Halothane concentration: 1.5-2.5%
                     Oxygen flow: 1 liter/minute
                     Nitrous oxide: 1 liter/minute
     Recovery: Turn off nitrous oxide and halothane
                 Flush system with oxygen
                 Keep bird on 100% O_2 until extubation

3. <u>Metafane</u>--very popular because of its low toxicity and wide margin of safety; longer induction period and longer recovery period than halothane.

            Induction: Place bird's head in mask
                        Metafane concentration: 3.5-4.0%
                        Oxygen flow: 2-3 liter/minute
                        Induction time: 8-10 minutes
          Maintenance: Intubate large birds/keep mask on small birds
                        Metafane concentration: 1.5-2.0%
                        Oxygen flow: 0.5-1.0 liter/minute

Metafane can be administered as a liquid directly to the bird, via TB syringe, a drop at a time near the nares or into the mouth. The metafane is absorbed through the mucous membranes and should be given to effect.

In each of these regimes a reduced oxygen flow may be appropriate for small birds. Also, after induction, the endotracheal tube will pass more easily if the bird's tongue is pulled forward with forceps. Once anesthetized, the bird's wings and legs can be taped to the operating table to secure it for surgery. Of course, the bird should not be placed directly on a cold table and should be kept warm throughout anesthesia.

Often vomiting, regurgitation, and aspiration pneumonia are a problem since birds are not fasted prior to surgery. These problems can be avoided if soft polyethylene tubing is inserted into the esophagus after induction. If vomiting or regurgitation occurs, ingesta will pass to the outside through this tube.

GENERAL ANESTHESIA--INJECTABLE

The injectable agents recommended are various combinations of ketamine, rompun, acepromazine, and valium. Intravenous sodium thiamyal (Surital) is effective, but hypothermia is severe and rapid. Also, recovery is prolonged, preventing the bird from eating and drinking soon after surgery. Equithesin, a mixture of chloral hydrate, magnesium sulfate, and pentobarbital, is very safe and reliable, but this product is difficult to obtain commercially; you can mix it up yourself, however. No matter what drug you use, the dose must be exact because once it's in the bird you can't get it back. You must know the precise weight of the bird in grams. As a guide, the average parakeet weighs 30 grams and the average canary weighs 20 grams. Small birds can be immobilized for weighing by wrapping them in a paper towel, while larger birds may have to be placed in a light cardboard cylinder or wrapped in a towel.

Injectable anesthetic agents, out of convenience, are usually delivered intramuscularly into the pectoral muscles. Often the dose required is so small that a microliter syringe must be used or the agent diluted tenfold in saline (1 part agent to 9 parts saline) and a TB syringe used. This dilution method presents a volume problem in small birds, however.

The injectable anesthetic regimes are listed below:

1. <u>Ketamine</u>--a dissociative anesthetic which apparently provides surgical anesthesia in birds. Ocular, oral, and swallowing reflexes are present, the eyes remain open and muscle tone increases. An overdose of ketamine produces tremors, convulsions, and death. Induction is usually smooth, with only a slight degree of excitement. Recovery, however, is characterized by a distinct excitatory phase of wing flapping and tremors which is very rough, in our opinion. The bird should definitely be wrapped for its own protection. In addition, fluid therapy may be required for long anesthetic episodes since ketamine is eliminated via the kidneys. Ketamine is available in a concentration of 100 mg/cc.

Small Bird Dosage: (all birds less than 500 gm)
   a. 1 mg/30 gm parakeet (0.01cc) or .033 mg/gm IM or
       33 mg/kg IM
       (1) Induction time: 30 minutes
       (2) Surgical plane: sedation only
       (3) Recovery period: 20 minutes
   b. 2 mg/30 gm parakeet (.02cc) or .067 mg/gm IM or
       67 mg/kg IM
       (1) Induction time: less than 3 minutes
       (2) Surgical plane: 5-12 minutes
       (3) Recovery period: 20-30 minutes
   c. 3 mg/30 gm parakeet (0.03 cc) or 0.1 mg/gm IM or
       100 mg/kg
       (1) Induction time: 2 minutes
       (2) Surgical plane: 20 minutes
       (3) Recovery period: 40-90 minutes
       (4) This is the maximum dose before signs of toxicity
            appear.

The LD_{100} of ketamine is 0.5 mg/gm (15 mg/30 gm bird).

To make recovery smoother, 1 cc of acepromazine (20 mg) can be mixed with a 10 ml vial of ketamine. The dose of ketamine is then calculated as if the acepromazine were not present.

Large Bird Dosage: (over 500 gm)
   a. 25-50 mg/kg IM
   b. Induction time: 1-5 minutes
   c. Surgical plane: 30 minutes - 6 hours, depending on the
       dose
   d. Additional injections for maintenance: 10 mg/kg IM or
       switch to gas anesthesia

2. <u>Ketamine and Rompun (Xylazine)</u>--this combination is preferred over ketamine alone because induction and recovery are smoother (but still somewhat rough). The regular dose of ketamine is halved, an equal volume of xylazine mixed in, and the dose administered intramuscularly:

Dose: Ketamine (100 mg/ml)
       .05 mg/gm or 1.5 mg/30 gm bird (.015 cc)
       Rompun (20 mg/ml)
       .01 mg/gm or 0.3 mg/30 gm bird (.015 cc)

In this formulation you will note that the dose of rompun is one-fifth the dose of ketamine, but the volumes of both are the same. Induction time, time in surgical plane, and recovery time are similar to those achieved by the 3 mg per bird dose of ketamine used alone.

We do not recommend using rompun alone. Although it offers good anesthesia, it is not reliable. It may also cause muscle tremors, bradycardia, partial A-V block, and a decreased respiratory rate. Pigeons experience adverse reactions to this drug.

Finally, we are aware of unpublished reports concerning the administration of diazepam (valium) during early recovery to smooth out the excitatory features. Valium apparently has been used in this manner with ketamine alone and with the ketamine/xylazine mixture. We have no data or experience regarding the dose of valium to be used.

ANESTHETIC EMERGENCIES

Several types of problems can develop during general anesthesia with either inhalational or injectable agents. In birds, these emergencies are usually the result of placing the bird in too deep a plane of anesthesia. For sure, dealing with them is not as easy or as successful as in small mammals. Your best defense against these crises is to know what they are and constantly watch for them, taking immediate action when they occur.

1. Apnea--observed during induction or recovery due to the accumulation of a volatile anesthetic in the air sacs, which act only as a reservoir for gases and have no absorptive function. To prevent apnea, maintain a good flow of oxygen during both induction and early recovery.

2. Respiratory arrest--immediately discontinue administration of the anesthetic (turn off the halothane or metafane). Administer 100% oxygen via endotracheal tube or face mask. If respiratory arrest lasts for more than 5 seconds, begin artificial respiration using slight digital pressure (thumb and forefinger) on the sternum at the rate of two per second. An IM injection or doxapram, .007 mg/gm (0.21 mg/30 gm bird), may also help.

3. Cardiac arrest--usually occurs simultaneously with respiratory arrest and if you are not monitoring the heart beat with an EKG or contact microphone, you won't know its happening. Again, you should turn off the anesthetic and administer 100% oxygen. Cardiac massage is accomplished using the same thoracic digital pressure applied during artificial respiration. Birds in cardiac arrest usually die.

4. Some anesthetized birds relax their tongue to such an extent that it falls back over the glottis. Breathing becomes impossible and the bird dies before you know it. If the bird is large enough, tracheal intubation will solve this problem. In smaller birds the tongue can be pulled forward and fixed to the lower beak with a paper clip.

QUESTIONS

1. Should a caged bird be fasted prior to anesthesia? Why?
2. What emergencies may arise during anesthesia?
3. What other problems, not considered emergencies, may occur during anesthesia?
4. What point must you keep in mind when anesthetizing weak, debilitated birds?
5. How can you protect a bird during recovery from anesthesia?
6. What areas of a bird's body are the most sensitive to painful stimuli?
7. What local anesthetics are used for birds?
8. What is the significance of the local anesthetic procaine with respect to birds?
9. Briefly describe the 3 stages of anesthesia.
10. How is the depth of anesthesia assessed in birds?
11. Which reflexes are most reliable in assessing the degree of anesthesia?
12. How does a bird under anesthesia breathe when it starts getting too deep?
13. What two basic types of general anesthesia are used in caged birds?
14. What inhalational anesthetic agent can be deposited in the mouth or near the nares and given to effect?
15. How can you induce general anesthesia in a mean bird which you cannot capture?
16. When using a gas anesthesia machine, what type of system must be employed, open or closed? Rebreathing or non-rebreathing?
17. What agents are used in the three inhalational regimes described?
18. What dose of ketamine is required for a 20-minute surgical procedure? Give mg/gm, mg/30 gm bird, and volume/30 gm bird.
19. What is the LD_{100} of ketamine in mg/gm for caged birds? How many times greater is the LD_{100} than the anesthetic dose?
20. What is the dose for ketamine and rompun when used in combination? Give mg/gm of each, mg/30 gm bird for each and volume/30 gm bird for each. What are the relative proportions by weight and by volume of each drug?

CHAPTER 15

FIRST AID FOR BIRDS

The first aid measures in this section are specific in most instances, but some general measures are often helpful for a variety of problems. Three non-specific therapeutic tools are described below, followed by a listing of specific problems and treatments.

1. Provide a nonstressful environment

    a. Quiet: no dogs or cats; no other birds which might compete for food, water, or territory
    b. Heat; 85-90°F
    c. No drafts
    d. Soft, circadian light (light which follows the regular daily cycle of light from the sun)
    e. Sufficient, accessible fresh water and food
    f. Let the bird rest

2. Gavage starving or anorexic birds

    a. Gevral protein concentrate mixed in warm hypoallergenic baby formula
    b. Place directly into crop with gavage apparatus
    c. Feed adults every 6-8 hours
    d. Feed nestlings and adolescents every 4-6 hours
    e. Do not feed if crop has not emptied or sour crop will develop

3. Nebulize once or twice a day for one hour

PROBLEMS WITH SPECIFIC FIRST AID MEASURES

Problem	Cause	First Aid Treatment
Respiratory problem: cough, sneeze, wheeze, click, nasal discharge	Infectious agent Air sac mites Tracheal worms Thyroid hyperplasia	1. See your vet immediately for this problem or bird will die soon 2. Nonstressful environment 3. Nebulization
Vomiting	Neurotic regurgitation Regurgitation of normal courtship behavior Crop or stomach disease Nestlings – food too coarse Parents – inexperienced	1. If behavioral, change environment 2. Nonstressful environment, especially heat 3. For GI infection: peptobismol and tetracycline orally 4. For minor obstructions: few drops of mineral oil by gavage 5. Provide parents with soft foods for nestlings
Diarrhea	Infectious agent GI parasite Spoiled food Abdominal tumor Nervous over-consumption of water	1. Nonstressful environment 2. Oral kaopectate and tetracycline 3. Stool sample to vet for flotation and culture 4. Monitor water consumption 5. Remove spoiled or watery ration
Sour Crop/bloated crop	Too much food too often to nestlings In adults: overeating or secondary to upper GI obstruction	1. Hold bird upside down and gently milk out stale crop contents 2. Flush mouth with warm water and bicarbonate of soda 3. Gavage – place bicarbonate solution into crop to neutralize acidity 4. Attempt to eliminate any obstruction 5. Offer fresh food only when crop is empty.
Passing undigested, whole seed	Gizzard atrophy Grit not provided Enteritis	1. See therapy for diarrhea 2. Provide adequate grit
Weight loss/wasting	Poor nutrition Parasitism Systemic disease	1. Good palatable diet and vitamin supplement 2. Oral antibiotic (tetracycline) 3. Nonstressful environment 4. If anorectic, gavage
Bone fracture	Trauma Calcium deficient diet Vit D_3 deficiency	1. Splint – masking tape plus support (tongue depressor, soda straw, pipe cleaner, plastic coffee stirrer) 2. Wing fx: tape wing to body (do not immobilize sternum); leave unaffected wing free
Broken toenail	Trauma Excessive length to nail	1. Grind or file down 2. Styptic pencil, silver nitrate stick, or pressure to stop bleeding

(cont.)

Problem	Cause	First Aid Treatment
Laceration	Trauma from: 1. combat 2. unsafe environment	1. Remove feathers from periphery of wound and treat as you would in humans 2. Clean with soap and water 3. Apply pressure to stop bleeding 4. Apply first aid cream 5. If sutures needed, see your vet 6. Always observe regularly when introducing new birds
Feather picking	Boredom Emotional disturbance Lack of privacy Endocrine or dietary imbalance Feather mites	1. Ensure normal routine is maintained 2. Provide regular diversion (human company) 3. Provide a balanced diet 4. Use Elizabethan collar if problem is severe 5. See vet for suspected mites or systemic disease
Broken, bleeding feathers	Trauma (self-inflicted, combat, or cage accident)	1. Remove remaining feather stub, including the portion in the follicle, with forceps or tweezers
Oil-soaked feathers	Excessive oil-base ointment Petroleum product contamination	1. Keep warm; rehydrate by gavage if dehydrated 2. Dissolve heavy oil with mineral oil 3. Remove light oil by several washings with Lux Liquid Amber^R detergent in warm water (15% solution) 4. Dry with hair dryer 5. Nonstressful environment
Egg-bound (signs include straining and duck-like posture)	Atonic or spastic uterus due to: 1. Calcium deficiency 2. Chilling 3. Infected uterus 4. Overbreeding 5. Out-of-season breeding 6. Old age 7. No nest provided 8. Obesity 9. Poor diet 10. Lack of exercise	1. Heat environment to 85-90°F 2. Mineral oil enema 3. See vet if egg is not passed within one hour
Poisoning	Lead-based paints Most houseplants Insecticides Cleaning agents	1. Nonstressful environment 2. Gavage with activated charcoal/mineral oil mixture (½ tsp/2 cc oil) 3. See vet
Eye problems	Trauma Infectious agent 1. Pox 2. Mycoplasma Chemical irritant	1. Flush eye with cool salt solution (2 tspn salt to 1 qt water) using eye dropper 2. Apply eye ointment for soothing effect 3. See vet immediately

CHAPTER 16

SAVING AND CLEANING OILED BIRDS

In this discussion we will assume that the bird most likely to be contaminated by oil and petroleum by-products will be a wild sea bird or an estuary bird. You may, however, see some caged and aviary birds whose feathers are soiled by excessive use of oil-based ointments.

GENERAL CONSIDERATIONS PRIOR TO CLEAN-UP
1. Be aware that wild birds harbor many zoonotic infectious agents, such as Salmonella and Chlamydia. Do not create a health hazard by careless sanitation.
2. Securely restrain wild birds and certain caged birds. Never leave the head and beak free. Always hold these birds at waist level or below and away from your face. Wear safety goggles.
3. If certain criteria apply, euthanasia may be the most humane method of dealing with an oil-soaked bird. When large numbers of birds are contaminated, a triage system must be set up to determine which birds are most likely to survive if cleaned up. The criteria for possible euthanasia are as follows:
        a. Persistent hypothermia, even after rehydration with warm IV fluids or warm gavage solution.
        b. Severe emaciation.
        c. Signs of systemic disease.
        d. Traumatic injury.
Birds which are on the "Threatened or Endangered Species" list and therefore protected by state or federal law should not be euthanized unless they have no chance of surviving.
4. If a bird is selected for clean-up and rehabilitation, follow these rules prior to the actual cleaning procedure:
        a. Clear the nares and mouth of oil and debris immediately.
        b. Keep the bird warm at 85-90°F; the environment should be draft-free. Oil-soaked feathers have no insulation effect, preventing the bird from conserving body heat.
        c. Do not stress the bird by
            (1) overcrowding
            (2) providing irregular lighting

          (3)   stimulating or frightening the bird with
                unnecessary human activity
    d. Check for signs of oil toxicity:
        (1)   red, inflammed skin
        (2)   loss of equilibrium
        (3)   Conjunctivitis
            Place a water-based ophthalmic ointment
               (Lacrilube[R]) in the eyes and on severely
               inflammed areas of the skin for protection dur-
               ing cleaning.
    e. Dehydrated birds should be rehydrated by gavage with
        25 cc/lb (50 cc/kg) of one of the following solutions:
        (1)   100 cc light Karo corn syrup in 1 qt water
        (2)   1 tspn table salt plus 50 cc of 50% dextrose in
             1 qt of fresh water

CLEANING PROCEDURE

1. Handle the soiled feathers gently.
2. Feathers must be thoroughly cleaned, rinsed, and dried. Even the smallest amount of oil residue left after cleaning will retard waterproofing.
3. Use the appropriate cleaning agent.
    a. Dissolve heavy oils with light mineral oil first, then use detergent.
    b. Light petroleum oils and mineral oil used in dissolving heavy oils can be removed with a detergent solution. A 15% concentration of Lux Liquid Amber[R] in warm water is generally an effective solvent.
4. Clean the bird with multiple detergent washings.
    a. Line up 3-6 basins filled with warm detergent solution.
    b. Gently dip the bird into the basin and slosh the detergent solution over the bird. Squeeze the solution out of the feathers by stroking the feathers in the direction of their normal contour.
    c. Spend about one minute in the first basin and 2-3 minutes in subsequent basins until the bird is clean.
5. Rinse the bird using a flexible hose with a shower head (water at 110°F should be directed against the normal lie of the feathers to remove all detergents).
6. Dry the bird with a dry towel or clean, dry rags.
7. Blow dry with a hair dryer or other warm air dryer.
8. Return to a nonstressful environment and force-feed, if bird will not eat on its own.

QUESTIONS

1. How would you dissolve heavy petroleum oils which have contaminated the plumage of a bird?

2. What detergent is recommended in this section for washing oil-soaked birds? What concentration?
3. How would you rehydrate a dehydrated bird covered with crude oil?
4. Briefly describe the cleaning process.

CHAPTER 17

THE CARE AND FEEDING OF ORPHANED BIRDS

Birds are developmentally classified after hatching as either precocial or altricial. Precocial birds include varieties such as chickens, duck, turkeys, and quail. At birth they possess soft, down feathers and juvenile wing feathers, and they are able to walk, drink, and forage short distances for food in the company of a parent. Altricial birds, on the other hand, are helpless at birth and require a long period of close parental care. They are naked, unable to walk, and must remain in the nest for protection against the elements and predators. They also require a steady ration from doting parents. Raptors, songbirds, pigeons, and doves are examples of altricial birds.

If one of your clients finds an orphaned precocial bird, encourage him to take it in and care for it. The authors have met with considerable success raising orphaned Bobwhite quail and Mallard ducks. The experience is richly rewarding while demanding only a small amount of your time, and it can be accomplished by a responsible child with minimal supervision.

A baby altricial, however, is another story. Its best chance for survival without question is with its natural parents. If, for example, you see a songbird that you think has been abandoned, observe it for at least an hour to determine if it really has been abandoned. It may be learning to fly and is simply resting between flight tests. During these rest periods it will receive food and coaching from its parents until it does learn to fly. Rarely do parents of altricial birds abandon their young. If the bird is very young and has obviously fallen from its nest, locate the nest and put the nestling back. There is absolutely no truth to the popular myth that parent birds will not accept offspring once they have been handled by humans. Rejection is not a problem since birds have a very poor sense of smell.

The fundamental problem with raising orphaned altricial birds is the availability of time. An orphaned songbird will need to be fed every 20 minutes during daylight hours and less frequently during the night for several weeks. There can be no missed feedings or the bird will die. This is not a job for a child or a mildly interested adult, and even with the best of efforts the results are often unsuccessful.

147

As a practitioner you should assess your client's desire, ability, and resources and then offer one of three options. The first is to return the bird to where it was found and let nature take its course. The second is euthanasia, which may prove the most humane option. The third option is to have a go at raising the orphaned bird. This path should be considered only if the client's concern for the orphan is genuine and if the client has ample free time and needs little sleep.

In addition, make a real effort to identify the species of bird since harboring a protected bird (or euthanizing one), no matter what the circumstances or how good your intentions, may be illegal. For accurate information regarding birds protected by law, contact your state wildlife department.

IMMEDIATE CARE

Quite likely a truly orphaned bird will be debilitated, weak, and cold. These are life-threatening signs in young nestlings. To rehydrate the bird oral fluid therapy using a homemade formula of one teaspoon salt and three teaspoons Karo syrup to a quart of water is best. This solution must be administered by dropper, delivering 5-10 drops every 15 minutes until the bird revives. Be forewarned, however, that too much of this homemade glucose/electrolyte solution given too fast will cause a fatal osmotic diarrhea. Intravenous fluids are an alternative but bleeding at the site of venipuncture is a common problem. The hypothermia can be handled by wrapping the bird in a dry towel and placing it in a dry box under a 75 watt light bulb situated 1-2 feet above the bird. Use a thermometer and adjust the temperature around 90-95°F at the bird's level by moving the light up or down.

AGING THE ORPHANED BIRD

Aging an abandoned bird is not critical but it may help you determine exactly what diet you should offer. All birds, precocial and altricial, penetrate the eggshell during hatching by means of a highly specialized structure located on the tip of the beak called an egg tooth. Not really a tooth, the structure is a short, white keratin spike which points dorso-caudally. At the end of the incubation period the hatching bird will strike the inside of the shell with its head and beak, causing the egg tooth to penetrate and crack the shell. This process is called pipping. The deciduous egg tooth may remain on the beak for as long as three days after hatching. Using feathers as a guide for aging, you will observe that altricial birds are still naked at one week of age. By two weeks, pinfeathers cover most of the skin. Body feathers soon appear on the back and wings and then on the abdomen and breast. At three weeks the nestling will be fully feathered. Flying occurs between four and six weeks of age.

CARE OF THE PRECOCIAL BIRD

   Using a cardboard box which is large enough to provide one square
foot of floor space for every two nestlings, you can raise baby
Bobwhite quail, baby wild turkeys, or wild ducklings with considerable
ease and success. Small holes one-half centimeter in diamter should
be cut in the sides of the box for ventilation and the floor covered
with newspaper, although a rougher surface, such as one provided by
construction paper or a thin cardboard packing material, would be
better to prevent spraddle legs from developing (see Chapter 8). The
paper should be changed daily. For birds less than five days old
fresh water should be offered in a jar lid filled with rocks about one
centimeter in diameter. This drinking arrangement prevents the young
bird from drowning if it accidentally falls into the drinker. Older
birds can be watered with an inverted jar-type waterer without the
rocks. Of course, as the bird grows, more floor space is required to
prevent crowding.

   Starter or starter-grower mash or crumbles formulated for domestic turkeys is an ideal ration for baby precocial birds. You can use
chicken starter or starter-grower if turkey feed is not available.
These rations should be available at any agricultural feed store. The
ration should be placed in a jar lid or a shallow cardboard dish.
Sprinkling the mash or crumbles on the floor of the box is not a good
idea since the bird's toes, soiled with moist fecal material, will
quickly become coated with the ration. Other birds will then pick at
the toes, injure them and possibly promote cannibalism.

   Finally, to prevent drafts the box should be covered with a towel
or a piece of cardboard. A 60-75 watt light bulb suspended below this
box cover will develop adequate heat to keep the babies warm. The
light should be left on day and night for 4-5 weeks (precocial birds,
unlike altricial ones, sleep very well with a light on). As a general
rule, the temperature in the box should be 90-95°F during the first
week of life. The temperature should then be lowered 5°F each
succeeding week until a comfortable 75°F is reached. Watching the
young birds offers the best gauge of whether the heat is right in your
homemade brooder. If the birds are huddled together directly under
the light, they are too cold and the light should be lowered closer to
the floor. If the birds spend most of their time near the corners or
walls of the box, they are too hot and the light should be raised.
The whole idea is to provide a warm, dry, draft-free brooder with
fresh water and free choice food served up daily. At three weeks of
age throw a little grit and fine chicken scratch, a mixture of cracked
corn, wheat, oats, barley, and milo, on the floor. As the birds grow
older, you should offer larger sizes of scratch along with a balanced
milled poultry ration.

   Between eight and twelve weeks of age most precocial birds are
ready to return to their natural environment. A feeding station
should be established in the wild for a couple of weeks to give the
bird or birds nourishment for the time it takes to learn to forage for
food on their own. If you have handled the birds regularly during
early development, release to the wild may be a problem since some

socialization to man and some slight domestication will have occurred. Socialization will not be a problem if your interactions with the bird are limited to brief clean-up and feeding sessions.

CARE AND FEEDING OF ALTRICIAL BIRDS

A homemade brooder similar to the one described for precocial birds will do nicely for altricial birds but with some significant modifications. Instead of a flat paper floor, the altricial bird requires a nest of shredded newspaper or rags. Circadian light is also a must if you are to successfully return the bird to nature at maturity. This means your heat source, the 75 watt light bulb, will have to be turned off at night and replaced by a heating pad under or adjacent to the box. Careful monitoring and adjustment of temperature are critical to keep the bird from experiencing temperature stress. This can be accomplished by placing a thermometer at the level of the nestling. If the temperature exceeds 90°F, insulate the heating pad with towels until the temperature is right. Just like the precocial brooder, the altricial brooder must be placed in a quiet, draft-free room and kept clean and dry.

Several rations have been described in the literature and one basic diet seems to appear for almost all altricial birds. The diet consists of two parts of a high quality, non-oily canned dog food, such as Hill's Prescription Diet, mixed thoroughly with one part crushed hard-boiled egg and one part canned chopped spinach which has been drained. A pinch of powdered milk and a drop of a multivitamin supplement may be added. The ration should be fluid enough to be drawn into a dropper but not runny. If the preparation is too thick, a very small amount of water may be added, although the juice from the spinach would be better. If the ration is too thin, a crushed soda cracker will bring the ration back to a proper viscosity. A baby altricial bird should never be given water until it is able to drink by itself. The ration described above will meet the nestlings water needs quite satisfactorily. Finally, while this diet should be prepared daily and refrigerated through the day to arrest spoilage, it must also be warmed before each feeding.

For the songbirds, the initial feedings may have to be accomplished with the nestling in your hand since it may resist eating, requiring you to pry open its mouth with tweezers. The nestling will soon understand what you are up to and reflexly gape to receive its meal on the end of a wooden stick or Q-tip. It will stop gaping when it has had enough to eat. It is best, however, to handle the bird as little as possible and feed it from the nest.

Nestling pigeons, called squab, and nestling doves are unique as altricial birds because they have the ability to suck. Were they not orphaned, their parents, both mother and father, would provide a white semi-fluid known as crop milk for the nestling to suck from their mouth and oropharynx. This crop milk is a secretion of the crop mucosal epithelial cells which swell and rupture, releasing the nutritious semi-fluid. To approximate crop milk the basic altricial ration can

be made slightly more fluid with warm homogenized milk. This modified
formula can be be administered to the nestling with the bulb from an
eye dropper, exercising care to apply constant pressure to the bulb
to make the ration constantly available at the open end. The nestling
will eagerly probe the dropper bulb and suck out its meal.

Some general feeding rules for altricial birds are listed below:

1. Very young nestlings require frequent feeding. Start out
feeding every 20-30 minutes during the day (sunup to sundown) and
every 1-2 hours at night. As the bird grows the frequency of feedings
will decrease.

2. When a bird is no longer hungry, it will stop gaping and
refuse food. If you are feeding it too often, it will resist your
efforts.

3. If the crop contains food from an earlier feeding, delay the
next meal until the crop is empty. This measure prevents development
of sour crop which results from the fermentation of the food stored
in the crop.

4. If the ration is too liquid, the bird may cry. Simply make
the ration more viscous by adding a crushed soda cracker.

5. Almost immediately after feeding, the nestling will back up
to the periphery of the nest and defecate. You should remove the
soiled rag or shredded paper just as the natural parents would.

6. If the ration soils the skin or feathers during feeding,
clean the nestling with a warm damp cloth so the insulation effect
will not be compromised.

7. Do not disturb the baby between feedings; let it rest.

As the nestling grows and matures the formulated ration can be
gradually withdrawn and replaced by a variety of seeds and other foods
in an effort to closely approximate what the bird will find in the
wild. It would be helpful but not necessary to determine whether the
bird is an insectivore or a seed-eater and make available the appropriate food. Grit is also essential to enhance the grinding action of
the muscular gizzard which is critical for the digestion of seeds or
breaking down the exoskeletal of some insects. The greater the dietary variety the bird experiences in captivity, the greater its chances
for a successful return to the wild. Table 17.1 offers a general list
of foods which can be offered between 3-6 weeks of age, a time when
the bird becomes fully feathered, eats and drinks on its own, leaves
the nest, exercises and tests it wings. When you observe this activity, move the bird to a cage in a room where the temperature is 75-
80°F. Provide water and feed dishes, sprinkle seed on the floor, and
install tree branches for perching.

TABLE 17.1. Foodstuffs Providing Dietary Variety for Altricial Birds

wild bird seed	mealworms	apple
chicken scratch	spiders	cherries
grass heads	ground beetles	sunflower seeds
chickweed	ants	grapes
crushed peanuts	breadcrumbs	hard-boiled egg

If the bird is not eating or drinking on its own, you will have to teach it by dropping food in front of it. Later, placing food around the cage and on branches teaches it to search for its food as it will have to do in the wild. Drinking can be taught by dipping the bird's beak into a shallow water dish. If the bird still hesitates, place bright colored marbles or small aluminum-foil balls in the feed and water dishes to arouse the bird's curiosity. It will peck at these attractions and discover it can be nourished at the same time.

At maturity, hang the cage in a window. When you see that the bird is eating well, acting restless and wild, and flying as best it can within the confines of its cage, release to the outdoors should be attempted. Give the bird every opportunity for success by choosing a day with tolerable weather and by ensuring that no predators are around. You should also provide a feeder until you are certain the bird can forage for itself. Most altricial birds will fly off with no difficulty, although a few will remain in the area of release for a week or so before moving on.

QUESTIONS
1. How are birds developmentally classified after hatching? Give examples of birds in each group.
2. What immediate care should be given to a cold, weak, and debilitated baby bird?
3. What is an egg tooth?
4. How would you make a homemade brooder for a precocial bird?
5. What would you feed a baby precocial bird?
6. What should the environmental temperature be for a one-day-old nestling?
7. How should the environmental temperature vary with the bird's age?
8. Describe how you would prepare the basic ration for an altricial nestling.
9. What is crop milk? Which birds produce crop milk?
10. How would you teach a bird to eat or drink?
11. Describe the differences between newly hatched precocial and altricial birds.
12. At what age do altricial birds become fully feathered? Begin to fly?
13. At what age are birds ready for release to the wild?
14. What are the chief reasons why a released bird does not successfully return to the wild?
15. How often does an altricial nestling need to be fed?

CHAPTER 18

THE POSTMORTEM EXAMINATION

A thorough necropsy will probably provide you with more information than any other diagnostic procedure. In fact, a diagnosis of diseases in poultry is often accomplished by gathering up several sick birds, sacrificing them, and subsequently performing a necropsy. This is not feasible, however, when dealing with individual caged birds or a flock of very expensive ones. As a practitioner, then, you will likely perform necropsies on birds which died on their own.

Experience will teach you that necropsies on autolytic birds or frozen birds are very unproductive. You must teach your clients that a diagnostic postmortem exam requires a bird which is only recently dead. Any time less than 12 hours dead is ideal, but some useful information can be obtained if you receive the bird as late as 1-2 days after death if you can tolerate the overwhelmingly offensive odor which will surely accompany such a bird. To preserve the bird as much as possible, it should be thoroughly soaked in water right down to the skin, placed in a plastic bag, and refrigerated. Often a client will just refrigerate the bird and later discover that the plumage insulated the bird well enough to permit autolysis to continue. So wet the bird down well. If the bird must be shipped, place the plastic bag with wetted bird inside in slush ice and use the fastest possible transportation. Never freeze a bird or pack it in dry ice.

Oftentimes a client will return from a weekend trip and find his bird dead. If the bird has started to decompose, advise him that a postmortem exam would be fruitless.

NECROPSY TECHNIQUE

TO PROTECT YOURSELF FROM PSITTACOSIS, PUT GLOVES AND A MASK ON BEFORE YOU BEGIN.

First, examine the outside of the bird for any signs of bone deformity, skin lesions, feather defects, or exudate. The feathers around the vent may be pasted from diarrhea, or the plumage of the shoulder and back may be soiled with exudate if a bird with a nasal discharge has wiped it off there. The bird should then be placed on

153

its back, with wings and legs extended by taping them to the necropsy
table. The plumage, if not already wet, should be dampened to prevent
dry feathers from floating around and making visualization difficult.
This will also help prevent the spread of psittacosis.

HEAD EXAM

The next area to be examined is the head. The nares should be
closely scrutinized for signs of an exudate. If an exudate is
present, the beak can be cut transversely and the sinuses examined.
The oral cavity can be exposed by cutting longitudinally between the
angle of the mandible and upper jaw. Look for exudate, erosions,
ulcers, or foreign bodies.

The cranium may provide you with some very revealing information.
Dissect the skin away from the dorsum of the skull. If the bird was
frozen, subcutaneous hemorrhage is not significant. Likewise, a small
degree of hemorrhage between the bones of the skull in a freshly dead
bird is considered agonal, and therefore insignificant. But a large
amount of subcutaneous hemorrhage in a freshly dead bird should
suggest trauma of some kind. Such cranial trauma is very common in
birds which escape or in birds allowed to fly freely which become
frightened. They will fly right into a wall at top flight speed,
suffering brain and bone trauma. Many owners refuse to believe their
bird would ever fly into a wall, but the lesions do not lie.

Later, when you have finished examining the entire abdomen, you
can take the time required to expose the brain and view it for
lesions. By carefully rimming the skull cranially, laterally, and
caudally with a scalpel blade, the calvarium can be removed and the
brain itself examined. An organized clot nearly always points to
trauma in pet birds.

In the next step, the skin should be incised down the ventral
midline from the throat to the vent and dissected laterally on both
sides to expose the musculature.

EXAM OF THE NECK REGION

At this point, the outside of the trachea and crop can be examined. Samples of trachea can be taken for virus isolation or the
tracheal lumen can be swabbed for bacterial and mycoplasmal culture.
In small birds like the finch and parakeet, a single seed can occasionally be found at the entrance of the trachea, suffocating the bird.
The crop can be opened and examined for candidiasis, which produces a
thick white cheesy material in the lumen, or the amount and type of
food can be determined, giving some useful nutritional information.
A normal crop wall appears almost transparent.

The ribs and sternum can be palpated for signs of rickets or
deformity and the breast muscles examined for protozoal infection;
specifically toxoplasmosis or sarcocystis. Make a stab through the
abdominal musculature just caudal to the keel bone. With scissors,
cut to your left (the bird's right) and cranially, severing the ribs
at the midthorax level. Go as far as the first rib. Make a similar

cut with scissors to your right but extend the cut cranially to include the right clavicle and right pectoral muscles. Carefully avoiding the vessels around the heart and lung, dissect the pericardial sac and heart away from the sternum. At this point you will be able to reflect the sternum to the left, exposing the organs of the thorax and abdomen.

EXAM OF THE THORAX

Immediately observe the organs associated with the thoracic inlet. Enlarged thyroids (a normal thyroid measures .5-1 mm x 1-2 mm) strongly suggest goiter due to an iodine deficient diet, while enlarged parathyroids, which normally are too small to see, indicate a calcium deficient diet. The trachea should be opened and its bifurcation examined for a tracheal plug or inspissated exudate from a respiratory condition. The muscular syrinx at the base of the trachea can also be identified. Inflammation of the syrinx is due either to <u>Aspergillus</u> or <u>Candida</u>.

Moving caudally, the pericardium is viewed for signs of inflammation, as are the thoracic air sacs. Exudative pericarditis, when accompanied by splenomegaly and airsacculitis, is highly suggestive of psittacosis. The heart should be examined for hemorrhage, hypertrophy and infarctions. Again, the ribs are in full view, only this time from the inside. Beneath the heart lie the lungs, rib crypts, the interclavicular air sacs, and a better view of the thoracic air sacs.

EXAM OF THE ABDOMEN

Leaving the heart and lungs and moving caudally, the liver will be seen covering the gizzard, and the abdominal air sacs will be seen caudal to the liver. Bacterial granulomas, tumors, fatty change, and the multifocal, necrotizing hepatitis of Pacheco's disease are the most common lesions observed in the liver. At this point in the necropsy you should take samples of air sac, pericardium, lung, and liver for histopathology and culture.

To get to the gizzard, spleen and the remainder of the GI tract, dissect and remove the portions of the liver which were not sampled. The gizzard can now be removed by dissecting and cutting its fascial attachment to the cloacal portion of the bird. Deflect the freed gizzard to the left and look for the proventriculus lying anteriorly in the alimentary canal. The spleen will be attached to the bottom of the gizzard. Never overlook the spleen. A discolored spleen may suggest a septicemia, a mottled, white spleen may indicate RE cell hyperplasia or a tumor, and splenomegaly points to psittacosis.

With the gizzard free, the small intestine, pancreas, and paired ceca can be pulled out of the abdomen easily. Carefully look for a pattern of intestinal hemorrhage (coccidiosis, nonspecific enteritis, Newcastle disease) and examine the lumen for catarrhal exudate, ingesta, and parasites. With the GI tract removed, the kidneys, ovaries or testes, and the adrenal glands can now be viewed along with the caudal aspect of the lungs and the abdominal cavity itself.

Routine necropsies often stop at this point, but much more can be learned with little more investigation:

1. Remove the kidneys and examine the lumbosacral plexus and the sciatic nerve. Also examine the brachial plexus. Yellow, swollen peripheral nerves may indicate a riboflavin deficiency or a neuritis. Histopathology would help determine which.

2. Open the major joints, looking for exudate or arthritic changes.

3. Cut the head off the femur to obtain marrow. A smear of bone marrow, when examined by a trained avian histopathologist, provides considerable diagnostic information concerning blood cell disorders. The bone marrow also offers the least contaminated material for bacterial or virus isolation.

Finally, the carcass should be disposed of by incineration, or chemically disinfected and discarded.

Table 18.1 summarizes the gross lesions specific to caged and aviary birds.

QUESTIONS
1. What is the best time (hours after death) to necropsy a bird?
2. If a dead bird must be stored for later necropsy, what is done to prevent autolysis?
3. In shipping a dead bird, what is the preferred method of refrigeration?
4. How do you stabilize a small pet bird on the necropsy table?
5. Why is the plumage wetted down prior to a necrospy?
6. State from memory the major sequential steps in performing a necropsy. Include only major areas of the bird in your description.
7. What will examination of the ribs and sternum tell you?
8. What should you look for when examining the following organs of caged birds?
    a. Breast muscle
    b. Thyroids
    c. Parathyroids
    d. Crop
    e. Subcutaneous tissue of the head
    f. Brain
    g. Spleen
    h. Hock
    i. Intestine
    j. Liver
    k. Pericardium
    l. Air sacs
9. What is a common cause of death in birds allowed to fly freely in a house?

TABLE 18.1.   The Postmortem Exam: Gross Lesions Specific to Caged Birds

ORGAN	LESIONS	POSSIBLE CAUSE
Skin	Proliferative crusts on legs, feet, and face, chronic dermatitis around vent	Cnemidocoptes pilae
	Lumps and bumps	Lipoma; other tumors
	Frayed feathers	French molt, poor nutrition, trauma, feather mites
	Yellow SQ nodules - legs	Gout
	Focal necrotic dermatitis	Idiopathic gangrene
Nares	Exudate	Respiratory disease; consider psittacosis
Eyes, mouth	Erosions, crusts	Avian pox
Beak	Deformed	C. pilae, no cuttlebone, trauma, poor nutrition
Feet	Abscessed pads, broken down	Staph infection, perch is wrong diameter
Crop	Thickened wall with white, cheesy contents	Candida, Trichomonas
Thyroid	Hyperplasia	Iodine deficiency
Parathyroid	Enlarged	Calcium or Vit D_3 deficiency
Pericardium	Cloudy, exudate present	Bacterial infection or psittacosis
Air sacs	Cloudy, exudate present	Psittacosis; mycotic, bacterial or mycoplasmal airsacculitis
Brain	Hemorrhage (organized clot)	Trauma
Liver	Multifocal necrosis with hemorrhage	Pacheco's disease, bacterial hepatitis, aflatoxin
	Fatty change, cirrhosis	
Spleen	Splenomegaly	Psittacosis
Kidneys	Yellow colored, hemorrhage, swollen, white streaks (urates)	Nephritis or nephrosis (many causes in pet birds)
Intestine	Hemorrhage, enteritis	Parasitism; Newcastle disease; bacterial, hemorrhagic, mycotic or simple enteritis
Lung	Focal consolidation	Aspergillus
Syrinx	Inflammatory exudate	Aspergillus, Candida
Trachea	Seed at entrance	Suffocation
	Tracheal plug, inflammation, exudate	Bacterial, viral, mycoplasmal infection
	Worms	Syngamus trachea

APPENDICES

(Authors give their permission for the following forms (pages 160-65)
     to be copied.)

AUTO HISTORY FORM

1. What symptoms does your bird show?

2. When did these symptoms first appear?

3. How frequently do these symptoms appear?

4. In your opinion, what is your bird's chief problem? What caused it?

5. Is there any previous history of illness?

6. Are there any recent medications or therapy?

7. Do cagemates show any signs?

8. Any new additions to your aviary or pet bird family? If so, what species? What age? When were they introduced? Where did they come from?

9. Have there been recent changes in environment?

	Yes	No
10. Activity normal?	___	___
Ability to fly normal?	___	___
Walking and perching normal?	___	___
Listless?	___	___
Restless?	___	___
Shifting weight from one foot to the other?	___	___
Any lameness or limping?	___	___
Squatting on perch or floor?	___	___
Straining as if to defecate?	___	___
Wings held away from body?	___	___
Head drawn back into chest?	___	___
Sits crouched with feathers ruffled?	___	___
Stretching?	___	___
Shivering?	___	___
Fainting?	___	___
Does the tail bob up and down?	___	___
Eyes closed or partly closed?	___	___
Any enlargements or change of the skin or legs?	___	___
Any vomiting or regurgitation? If yes, do you see mucus or seed?	___	___

11. Appetite: NORMAL or ABNORMAL? If abnormal, is your bird eating
              MORE or LESS?

12. Describe your bird's diet.

13. Is there a craving for a particular food, grit, paper, or plant?

14. What supplements are given? Vitamins? Minerals?

15. How much water does your bird drink each day?

16. Droppings: Normal   Abnormal

     Consistency → firm   loose   watery

     Color → _____

17. Breathing: Normal   Abnormal
     (Circle those that apply)

     Noisy   Nasal discharge   Squeaks
     Fast   Sneezing   ↓ Talking
     Labored   Choking

18. Feathers: Normal   Molting   Scratching   Picking

19. What is your bird's breeding history?

CHECKLIST FOR EXAMINATION OF THE CAGE

1. General level of sanitation.

2. Husbandry: correct size cage?   proper accessories?
                is cage safe?   any painted surfaces?
                toys safe?

3. Perches: Diameter
              Surface - smooth or rough?
              Cleanliness
              Height in cage

4. Droppings: Number   Odor
                Color   Consistency

5. Diet: is bird eating?   vegetables, greens, fruits fresh?

           what is bird eating?   supplements?

6. Grit: size and amount

7. Cuttlebone: used?   Oystershells present?

8. Dishes (water, feed, treats):   big enough?   clean?

9. Mites present?   cuttlebone band, ends of perches, frayed cage
                    cover

10. Feathers on floor: molting?   excitement?

11. Mirrors: signs of regurgitation?

PHYSICAL EXAM FORM

Owner_____ Bird's name_____

Type of Bird_____ Sex_____ Color_____

PERTINENT HISTORY:

CHIEF COMPLAINT:

EXAMINATION:

    Head: Eyes_____

            Cornea_____

            Pupillary response_____

            Eyelids_____

            Cere (color)_____

            Nares_____

            Tongue_____

            Mouth_____

            Beak_____

            Larynx_____

            Respiratory sounds_____

            Ears_____

    Neck: Crop_____

  Thorax: Sternum_____

            Musculature_____

            Respiration_____ Rate_____ Depth_____

            Auscultation

  Abdomen: Distance from sternum to pelvis (5 mm is normal in

            parakeet)_____

            Palpation_____

            Vent_____

    Legs_____

    Feet_____

    Nails_____

    Wings_____

    Feathers_____

    Skin_____

General Condition:_____

    Conformation_____

    Attitude_____

    Weight_____

    Posture_____

    Droppings

    Color_____

    Odor_____

    Consistency_____

    PCV_____ Plasma Protein_____

PROBABLE DIAGNOSIS:

RX:

INSTRUCTIONS TO AN OWNER TAKING HIS BIRD HOME FROM THE HOSPITAL

1. Remove grit from the bird's cage.

    a. In the excitement of returning home, a bird may overeat grit.
    b. Sick birds often develop a depraved appetite and engorge themselves on grit, resulting in impaction of the gizzard and proventriculus. Grit, unlike minerals, does not dissolve in the GI tract.

    c. Wait a week and then offer grit in the mineral/salt dish which the bird usually eats from only occasionally during the day. After several weeks grit may be placed on the floor or in a dish by itself.

2. Provide a nonstressful environment.

    a. Keep the dog and cat away.

    b. Separate from other birds to prevent competition for food, picking, and fighting.

    c. Temperature should be 80-90°F.

    d. Environment should be quiet.

    e. Provide circadian light but daylight should be dimmer than normal.

    f. No drafts.

3. Allow the bird to rest. Darkness during daylight hours will help the bird to get more sleep but he will not eat or drink in the dark. A dimly lit, quiet cage, therefore, is recommended.

4. Medicate as directed.

5. Monitor stool - keep a written record.

    a. Number of droppings.

    b. Consistency.

6. Estimate daily water consumption.

BIBLIOGRAPHY

AAHA Committee Report. 1963. Drugs and dosages in budgerigars. <u>J. Small Anim. Pract.</u> 4:27.

Altman, R. B., ed. 1973. Cage birds. <u>Vet. Clin. North Amer.</u> 3(2): 143-236.

————. 1979. Avian clinical pathology, radiology, parasitic, and infectious diseases. In <u>AAHA's 46th Annual Meeting Proceedings</u>, pp. 15-27.

————. 1980. Avian anesthesia. <u>Compend. Cont. Ed. Pract. Vet.</u> 2(1): 38-43.

Arnall, L. 1965. Conditions of the beak and claw in the budgerigar. <u>J. Small Anim. Pract.</u> 6:135-44.

Arnall, L., and Keymer, I. F. 1975. <u>Bird diseases.</u> Neptune City, N. J.: T.H.F. Pubns., Inc.

Bankowski, R. A., Arnstein, P., and Meyer, K. F. 1977. Psittacosis---Ornithosis. In <u>Current Veterinary Therapy VI</u> ed. R. W. Kirk, pp. 698-703. Philadelphia: Saunders.

Beach, J. E. 1962. Diseases of budgerigars and other cage birds. <u>Vet. Rec.</u> 74:10-15, 134-40.

————. 1965. Some of the major problems of budgerigar pathology. <u>J. Small Anim. Pract.</u> 6:15-20.

Blackmore, D. K. 1965. The pathology and incidence of neoplasia in cage birds. <u>J. Small Anim. Pract.</u> 6:217-23.

Blackmore, D. K., and Lucas, J. F. 1965. A simple method for the accurate oral administration of drugs to budgerigars. <u>J. Small Anim. Pract.</u> 6:27-29.

Boever, W. J., and Wright W. 1975. Use of ketamine for restraint and anesthesia of birds. <u>VM/SAC</u> 70(1):86-88.

Bostock, C. Life styles - parrots. <u>Atlanta Weekly</u> (July 20, 1980) pp. 10-11, 29.

Bruner, D. W., and Gillespie, J. H. 1973. <u>Hagan's Infectious Diseases of Domestic Animals.</u> Ithaca: Cornell U. Pr.

Cappuci, D., ed. 1972. <u>California pet bird surveillance report.</u> California State Department of Public Health.

Collins, D. R. 1973. Exotic psittacines. <u>VM/SAC</u> 68(4):368-73.

167

Cooper, R., and Howard, E. 1977. Inclusion body disease of psitta-
    cines. In Proceedings of the 26th Western Poultry Disease Confer-
    ence and 11th Poultry Health Symposium, pp. 21-24.
Docherty, D. E., and Henning, D. J. 1980. The isolation of a Herpes
    virus from captive cranes with an inclusion body disease. Avian
    Dis. 24(1):278-83.
Dolphin, R. E. 1977. Collecting and handling blood samples from small
    cage birds. VM/SAC 72(5):928-30.
————. 1977. Hospital care for birds. VM/SAC 72(4):641-43.
Dolphin, R. E., and Olsen, D. E. 1977. Anesthesia in the companion
    bird. VM/SAC 72(11):1761-65.
————. 1977. Antibiotic therapy in cage birds for pathogenic bacteria
    detected by fecal culture technique. VM/SAC 72(9):1504-7.
————. 1977. Fecal monitoring of cage birds. VM/SAC 72(6):1081-85.
————. 1977. The feeding and care of orphan birds. VM/SAC 72(12):
    1868-69.
————. 1977. Psittacosis and resistant infection in companion birds.
    VM/SAC 72(1):70-74.
————. 1977. Rapid postmortem examination of companion birds. VM/SAC
    72(7):1189-93.
————. 1978. Bacteriology of Companion birds. VM/SAC 73(3):359-61.
————. 1978. Restraint and physical examination of companion birds.
    VM/SAC 72(1):59-63.
Engholm, E. 1973. Bird infirmary. New York: Taplinger.
Erickson, G. A., Mare, C. J., Gustafson, G. A., Miller, L. D.,
    Proctor, S. J., and Carbrey, E. A. 1978. Interactions between
    viscerotropic velogenic Newcastle disease virus and pet birds of
    six species. I. Clinical and serological responses, and viral
    excretion. Avian Dis. 21(4):642-54.
Estudillo, J. 1977. A Newcastle disease outbreak in captive exotic
    birds. Unpublished. Mexico 13, D.F.
Fisher, N. A. 1980. Care of orphaned wild animals. Compend. Cont.
    Ed. Anim. Health Tech. 1(3):137-44.
Fowler, M. E. 1979. Care of orphaned wild animals. Vet. Clin. North
    Amer. 9(3):447-71.
Francis, D. W. Newcastle disease and psittacines, 1970-71. Poult.
    Dig. (Jan. 1973) pp. 16-19.
Friedburg, K. M. 1962. Anesthesia of parakeets and canaries. JAVMA
    141(10):1157-60.
Galvin, C. 1976. Avian drugs and dosages. Wildlife Rehabilitation
    Council of California.
Goodman, L. S., and Gilman, A. 1975. The pharmacologic basis of
    therapeutics. New York: Macmillan.
Graham, D. L., Transmission of Pacheco's Disease. Pet Bus. (Dec.
    1978) p. 8.
Harrison, G. J. 1978. First aid for birds. Unpublished. Lake Worth,
    Florida.
Hasholt, J. 1966. Diseases of the female reproductive organs of pet
    birds. J. Small Anim. Pract. 7:414-20.

Himmelstein, S., and Bernstein, K. 1978. Clinical aspects of nutritional secondary hyperparathyroidism in caged birds. VM/SAC 73(6): 761-63.

Hitchner, S. B., Domermuth, C. H., Purchase, H. G., and Williams, J. E., eds. 1975. Isolation and identification of avian pathogens. Ithaca: Arnold Printing Corp.

Hodges, R. D. 1974. The histology of the fowl. New York: Academic Pr.

Hofstad, M. S., ed. 1978. Diseases of poultry - 7th edition. Ames: Iowa St. U. Pr.

Hoge, R. S. 1966. Anesthesia and surgery for egg bound parakeets. Anim. Hosp. 2:46-47.

Humason, G. L. 1972. Animal tissue techniques. San Francisco: Freeman.

Ivens, V. 1965. Infestation of a parakeet with Knemidocoptes pilae. JAVMA 147(9):968-69.

Janovski, N. A. 1966. Disseminated aspergillosis in a Mynah bird. JAVMA 194(7):944-49.

Kalmer, G. 1975. Intranuclear inclusion bodies in an African Gray parrot. Avian Dis. 19(3):640-42.

Kastris, A. Trying your wings at bird-sitting. Virginia Wildlife (June 1980) pp. 15-16.

Kerlin, R. E. 1964. Venipuncture of small birds. JAVMA 144(8):870-74.

Keymer, I. F. 1961. Postmortem examinations of pet birds - I. Mod. Vet. Prac. 42(23):35-38.

————. 1961. Postmortem examinations of pet birds - II. Mod. Vet. Prac. 42(24):47-51.

King, A. S., and McLelland, J. 1975. Outlines of avian anatomy. Baltimore: Williams & Wilkins.

Kirk, R. W., ed. 1974. Current veterinary therapy V, pp. 553-86. Philadelphia: Saunders.

————. 1978. First aid for pets. New York: Dutton.

Lafeber, T. J. 1966. Feather problems in caged birds: the role of nutrition. Anim. Hosp. 2:199-204.

————. 1967. Feather problems in caged birds: relationship to the endocrine glands. Anim. Hosp. 3:49-51.

Leibovitz, L. 1962. Unusual bird-parasite cases and overall parasite incidence found in a diagnostic laboratory during a five year period. Avian Dis. 6(2):141-44.

Lucas, A. M., and Stettenheim, P. R. 1972. Avian anatomy-integument. USDA Handbook 362, vol. 1.

Mandel, M. 1977. Lincomycin in treatment of out-patient psittacines. VM/SAC 72(3):473-74.

Marshal, A. J., ed. 1960. Biology and comparative physiology of birds. New York: Academic Pr.

Mathey, W. J. 1967. Respiratory acariasis due to Sternostoma tracheacolum in the budgerigar. JAVMA 150(7):777-80.

Miller, T. D., Millar, D. L., and Nazi, S. A. 1979. Isolation of Pacheco's disease herpes virus in Texas. Avian Dis. 23(3):753-56.

Olsen, R. E., and Dolphin, R. E. 1978. Administering therapeutic
    agents to cage birds. VM/SAC 73(8):1045-50.
————. 1978. Parasitism in the companion bird. VM/SAC 73(5):640-44.
————. 1978. Virology 1: avian pox. VM/SAC 73(10):1295-97.
Panigraphy, B., Elissalde, G., Grumbles, L., and Hall, C. 1979.
    Giardia infection in parakeets. Avian Dis. 22(4):815-18.
Petrak, M. L., ed. 1969. Diseases of cage and aviary birds. Phila-
    delphia: Lea & Febiger.
Rogers, C. H. 1969. Parrot guide. Harrison, N. J.: Pet Libr. Ltd.
————. 1970. Parakeet guide. Harrison, N. J.: Pet Libr. Ltd.
Ridgeway, R. L. 1977. Oral xanthoma in a budgerigar, Melopsittacus
    undulatus. VM/SAC 72(2):266.
Schmidt-Nielson, K. 1971. How birds breath. Sci. Amer. 225(6):73.
Scott, M. L., Nesheim, M. C., and Young, R. J. 1976. Nutrition of
    the chicken. Ithaca: Scott.
Sheridan, K. 1979. Giardiasis, unpublished. Athens, Ga.
Simpson, C. F., and Hanley, J. E. 1977. Pacheco's parrot disease of
    psittacine birds. Avian Dis. 21(2):209-19.
Simpson, C. F., Hanley, J. E., and Gaskins, J. M. 1975. Psittacine
    herpesvirus infection resembling Pacheco's parrot disease. J.
    Infect. Dis. 131(4):390.
Smith, H. A., Jones, T. C., and Hunt, R. D. 1972. Veterinary
    pathology. Philadelphia: Lea & Febiger.
Soulsby, E. J. L. 1968. Helminths, arthropods, and protozoa of domes-
    ticated animals. Baltimore: Williams & Wilkins.
Spalatin, J., and Hanson, R. P. 1975. Epizootiology of Newcastle
    disease in waterfowl. Avian Dis. 19(3):573-82.
Steiner, C. V. 1980. The cardiac racing phenomenon in parakeets.
    VM/SAC 75(2):250.
Steiner, C. V., and Davis, R. B. 1979. Scaly-leg and face mite infes-
    tation in a parakeet. VM/SAC 74(7):965-68.
————. 1979. Thyroid hyperplasia in a parakeet. VM/SAC 74(5):739-42.
————. 1980. The significance of depression in caged birds. VM/SAC
    75(4):634-35.
Stunkard, J. A., and Miller, J. C. 1974. An outline guide to general
    anesthesia in exotic species. VM/SAC 69(9):1181-87.
Sturkie, P. D. 1954. Avian physiology. Ithaca: Comstock.
————., ed. 1976. Avian physiology. New York: Springer-Verlag.
Tierney, F., and Baillie, J. 1979. Malathion aerosol for treatment
    of scaly face mites in caged birds. VM/SAC 74(1):69-70.
Tribby, I., Friis, R., and Moulden, J. 1973. Effect of chlorampheni-
    col, bifampicin, and nalidixic acid on Chlamydia psittaci growing
    in L cells. J. Infect. Dis. 127:155-63.
USDA. 1978. Worth repeating - special rules for bringing pet birds
    into the United States. US Govt. Print. Off.
Wallach, J., and Flieg, G. 1969. Nutritional secondary hyperpara-
    thyroidism in captive birds. JAVMA 155(7):1046-51.
Williams, A. S. 1978. Saving oiled seabirds. International Bird
    Rescue Research Center and the American Petroleum Institute.

INDEX